# TWENTIETH CENTURY
# INTERPRETATIONS

Maynard Mack, *Series Editor*
Yale University

NOW AVAILABLE
*Collections of Critical Essays*
ON

TWENTIETH CENTURY
INTERPRETATIONS
OF
# ARROWSMITH

# TWENTIETH CENTURY
## INTERPRETATIONS
## OF
# ARROWSMITH

*A Collection of Critical Essays*

Edited by

ROBERT J. GRIFFIN

Prentice-Hall, Inc.  A SPECTRUM BOOK    *Englewood Cliffs, N. J.*

# Contents

# Introduction

## by Robert J. Griffin

In April of 1926 Sinclair Lewis was in Kansas City, Missouri, industriously compiling data for what was to be his hardest hitting and possibly least persuasive novel. He had already made good progress in the careful preliminary work of outlining the novel and constructing detailed dossiers of characters. Little wonder that it later became a cliché to compare his method of preparing for a novel with the work of a research scientist. No one would call the finished *Elmer Gantry* a scientific novel. Many still hesitate to call it a novel at all, and Mark Schorer has aptly defined its distorted fictive vision as the "method of half-truths." Yet *Arrowsmith*, Lewis's previous major work, very definitely is a novel, and one which takes as its subject the troubled career of a research scientist who cannot be satisfied with partial or unsubstantiated truth.

It must have seemed, that April, that *Arrowsmith* had already made its mark, but its current history as a public phenomenon had still one signal event to go. On April 25, Lewis was, as he put it, "offered" the Pulitzer Prize for his medical novel. Work on the religious novel would have to be put aside for a short time while he perfected his response to this problematical honor. His refusal was a gesture that Martin Arrowsmith could be proud of. "All prizes, like all titles, are dangerous," and Lewis explained the dangers he saw in the Pulitzer. For one, he cited the actual terms of the award, "for the American novel . . . which shall best present the wholesome atmosphere of American life"—the very existence of which Lewis had been trying to deny. For another, he deplored the possibility that this annual selection of the "best" novel should become "so rooted and so sacred" that novelists might, unconsciously or otherwise, write *for* the prize instead of for inherent excellence, and thus another compulsion for writers to be "safe, polite, obedient, and sterile" would be ceded pernicious authority.

Undoubtedly there was some personal animus involved in Lewis's refusal. *Main Street* had been selected by the Pulitzer literary jury for 1921; the Trustees of Columbia University quashed the jury's decision and gave the prize to Edith Wharton for *The Age of Innocence*. In

1922, the choice was *Alice Adams,* Booth Tarkington's "answer" to *Main Street,* and in 1923, the year *Babbitt* was eligible, the prize went to *One of Ours,* which is hardly the best of Willa Cather's work. Lewis hinted at his indignation when he noted that "the administrators can, and sometimes do, quite arbitrarily reject the recommendations of their supposed advisers." In an earlier letter to Alfred Harcourt (April 4, 1926) he had reminded his publisher that "ever since the *Main Street* burglary" he had made up his mind to refuse the award if it were ever offered to him. His refusal, however, was not purely a matter of hurt vanity or the intent to retaliate. He could not accept such an institutionalized seal of approval and remain true to the general vision expressed in Martin Arrowsmith's career.

Ultimately, to be sure, the comparison with the research scientist fails, because Lewis, for all his painstaking accumulation of data based on actual experience and observation, was willing to present his findings in deliberately slanted fictions that might appall a "pure" researcher. In this respect, he was more a Tubbs than an Arrowsmith, more a popularizer than an original discoverer or inventor. But if Lewis was capable at times of the most unabashed self-publicizing, he also had a strong streak of the Arrowsmithean in his character. Perhaps "Gottliebean" would be the more accurate term for his strain of unrelenting idealism. Lewis wrote a "Self-Portrait" in 1927 (noted in Richardson's essay) in which he remarked that his respect for learning, integrity, accuracy, and the possibilities of human achievement was expressed in the person of Gottlieb. Nevertheless it is Martin Arrowsmith himself who provides the closest parallel to his creator, for the very reason that he is an unheroically complex, often confused and faltering, rather selfish and unprofound person whose importance as a character does not depend on his fully succeeding in the quest to which he has dedicated his life.

In 1941, when Lewis wrote another self-portrait in the form of an ironic obituary, he called it "The Death of Arrowsmith," evidently without thinking it necessary to explain the identification implied in the title. Nor is the identification developed as a metaphor within the article. That is, Lewis uses his own name and tries to deal accurately with the facts of his career to date and the projected likelihoods of his old age, picturing himself—alas, inaccurately—retired peacefully to a small country place in New England. He recognizes that he may have been "an inevitably lone and insulated figure," and he draws on the old scientific analogy by calling himself an "experimental wanderer" and a "cheerful pathologist, exposing the clichés and sentimentalities of his day." Although this is not the place to determine the exact degree of his autobiographical involvement in *Arrow-*

*smith,* a sketch of Lewis's early life and subsequent literary career may suggest some of the points of parallelism.

Harry Sinclair Lewis was born in the village of Sauk Centre, Minnesota, February 7, 1885, the son, grandson, and nephew of practicing physicians. As it turned out, an older brother, Claude, was still practicing in St. Cloud, Minnesota, when Lewis died in Italy in 1951. In later years Lewis's public memories of his childhood gave off a rather rosy glow. The truth had been closer to the brown hues of *Main Street.* Young Harry Lewis was lanky and pimpled; almost never at ease and, without benefit of choice, a loner; an omnivorous reader and restless dreamer. He dreamed now of belonging—like Claude the all-around American boy—and now of escaping. At thirteen he tried to run off to enlist as a drummer boy in the Spanish-American War. Of course Dr. Edwin J. Lewis, an archetypally stern, self-sure, and unbending father, caught him at the train station; Harry had left a note.

Harry's mother died when he was six. The sensible, improvement-minded step-mother that Dr. E. J. married about a year later was probably the most sympathetic member of the family. She seems to have encouraged, for example, his "peculiar" appetite for reading. Not even she knew quite what to do about the frantic show-off child who never managed to shine in the eyes of his fellow villagers. In the last two years of high school, after a very poor record—poorest in Deportment—Harry became a serious student. He was still a troublesome prankster yearning for attention and, though he was able to get elected president for a semester of one of the small school's two literary societies, still unpopular, unsuccessful with the girls. But the dream of college had begun to afford at least a hope of stability as he floundered through more than the usual awkwardnesses of adolescence. In a life devoid of grace, devoid of substantial excitement, he had a hazy, Tennysonian vision of intellectual and aesthetic glory. "To read books," he wrote in his diary, "to gaze on pictures, to wander through green fields and stately woods and by sapphire water, ever ever thinking and progressing ever, though slowly or swiftly to the divine purity!" He had had one friend worth the name in Sauk Centre. (One remembers that Martin Arrowsmith is allowed only the sketchiest of childhoods, and by the time he gets to college at the beginning of chapter II, he has mysteriously lost both parents.)

Between high school and Yale, Harry attended the preparatory Academy at Oberlin College in Ohio. There he studied hard, suffered occasionally from homesickness, became much more seriously interested in religion, suffered occasionally from self-righteousness, and wrestled with the possibility of studying theology and becoming a foreign missionary. Another possibility was a life of scholarship, in history or literature. He found no friends at Oberlin. No matter; Yale was ahead, such stuff as dreams could build on.

He arrived at New Haven on September 18, 1903. If the sophisticates at Oberlin Academy had thought him a conceited and querulous rube, the Yalies' distaste may be imagined. Harry Lewis roomed alone. He was relegated to the company of other (the phrase is Mark Schorer's) "eccentric strays." But his professors, especially Chauncey Brewster Tinker, were more tolerant of the gawky, anxious red-head; and he did publish a joke in the *Yale Record* and one of his dreamily medievalistic poems—the kind he later called "Tennyson-and-water" —in the *Literary Magazine,* the first freshman effort accepted that year. He was also the first freshman poet published in the less prestigious *Courant,* which took five of his works before the year was out. When life offers little in the way of acceptance, might literature serve instead? He was still a serious, enthusiastic student and won honors both terms. He still read voraciously, and for a while worked part-time for a newspaper in New Haven, as he had back home in Sauk Centre.

After a summer cattle-boat trip to England that would later be used in *Our Mr. Wrenn,* Lewis returned to Yale and went into a bad sophomore slump—a sort of low-key Center of Indifference. The theological and missionary ambitions faded away and his grades declined. He did, however, continue to publish in the campus magazines, and he sold an article about a possible case of plagiarism to a national magazine, *The Critic.* The name on the article was Sinclair Lewis. He became interested in philosophical naturalism, resolved to pursue unromanticized "truth," to "study more biology, etc." He became more and more interested in socialism, too, but his personal ambition was now fixed on a literary career.

A dull summer in Sauk Centre was followed by a busy junior year in which Lewis was not only recognized as an outstanding campus nonconformist, but also elected to the editorial board of the *Lit.* He was also elected editor of the *Courant,* but declined, to devote his energies to polemical pieces in the *Lit*: attacking indifference to reading, complaining about the stuffiness of most student writing, defending undergraduate heresy. Meantime Lewis was acquiring a little social savoir faire and a larger measure of self-awareness. His many efforts to publish in national periodicals resulted only in the sale of a few poems for children. Another summer cattle-boat voyage to England, another year at Yale.

But no, in October of his senior year (1906), Lewis and Allan Updegraff left college to become janitors at Helicon Hall, Upton Sinclair's short-lived utopian community in New Jersey. The idealist fervor of the literary janitors lasted one month, after which they moved to New York to try the life of free-lance writing. Lewis was able to sell some of his work, mostly children's verse, and he got a regular job on the staff of *Transatlantic Tales,* translating French and German poetry and fiction into English. In the next several months he enjoyed his first serious courtship (the lady would later claim to be the model for Leora), made a brief foray into Panama, where he could find no work, and finally returned to Yale. He completed a whole year's work in one term and was graduated in June, 1908. He thought of going to graduate school to become a professor of English, but soon, wisely, rejected that possibility, as he had rejected the inevitable notion that he might follow in the family tradition of medicine.

By now he was sure that writing would be his life; exactly how he might make a living remained to be seen. Between 1908 and 1914, he was employed, off and on, in various parts of the U.S., as a newspaperman, secretary to a pair of lady novelists, sub-editor of a small journal for teachers of the deaf, publisher's reader and publicity writer, assistant editor of a pulp adventure magazine, and the main writer of a syndicated weekly book page. He now introduced himself as Sinclair Lewis. He published a few unnotable poems, short stories, articles and reviews, and a pseudonymous children's novel, *Hike and the Aeroplane*; he was working on a real novel.

*Our Mr. Wrenn: The Romantic Adventures of a Gentle Man* appeared in 1914. Lewis had met and frequently proposed to Grace Livingstone Hegger, a pretty young lady, literate, chic, and rather snobbish (their first quarrel erupted when she "froze" a boorish friend he had brought home for dinner). The novel was dedicated to her, and shortly after it was published, they were married. *The Trail of the Hawk: A Comedy of the Seriousness of Life* appeared in 1915. Neither novel sold well enough to allow Lewis to quit his latest job with George Doran's publishing firm, but the publication of several short stories in *Saturday Evening Post* did.

Resuming the life of restless travel, presumably no longer alone, he would never again be shackled to the horror of a "routine" job. Nothing would ever be routine: neither the first fitful marriage nor the second (to Dorothy Thompson, the famous journalist), each of which lasted about 14 years. There would be no peaceful retirement to rural New England, no slaking of the deep thirsts; there would be, for what it was worth, international fame. When Lewis was chosen for the Nobel Prize in 1930, he rather ingenuously observed that this was altogether different from the Pulitzer, since it honored the whole of a writer's work; besides, the handsome cash award would contribute to the upkeep of a struggling American author. Yet, in the midst of worldly success, he took the occasion to make a forceful speech about "The American Fear of Literature." One more uncompromising gesture that Arrowsmith could esteem.

Whatever else Sinclair Lewis was, he was not a brilliant flash in the pan. To be sure, he enjoyed international fame while relatively young —he was only 45 in 1930—and his reputation began to wane soon after the triumphant journey to Stockholm, partly because he never again wrote a novel as good as, say, *Arrowsmith* or *Babbitt*. But if his decline appears now to have been meteoric, his rise must still be judged slow. Young Lewis certainly wanted to be a writer, as thousands of lonely small-town girls want to be great actresses. At Yale he went through all the motions, but his creative contributions to the campus magazines are not perceptibly promising: they are for the most part undistinguished undergraduate writing, either flaccid or strained, "romantic" in the sense of sophomorically dreamy. He seems always to have had a story-teller's imagination (before he hit his stride as a professional writer, he used to sell plots to Jack London), and his early publications reveal some of the concerns that we find characteristic of the later works. The glimmer of great expectations, however, is faint at best; most likely it is seen only by virtue of the optical illusion we call hindsight. Lewis was slow to develop. Indeed, "develop" is inept, for Lewis was a writer less born than self-made. Though he never quite became the kind of impeccable literary craftsman that would satisfy a James Joyce, he was incontestably a dedicated artisan, a writer who worked at his trade with uncommon determination and perseverance, with ingenuous pride and ambition, and for a while, with notable success.

*Our Mr. Wrenn* is the story of a timid, solitary shoe-clerk who travels, matures, gradually becomes a fairly enviable average man, allowing Lewis to present some detailed images of modern American life, especially of metropolitan life as it pertains to clerks and boarding-house society. *The Trail of the Hawk* is a better written novel, and more emphatically American. Carl Ericson's peregrinations range over most of the continent, and Lewis apparently meant the course of his hero's life—from youth as a hyphenated American through pioneer adventuring as a vanguard aviator to industrial flair without loss of the questing spirit and capacity for frolic—to epitomize the progress of national history, part retrospect and part hopeful prophecy. Carl's marriage is underscored as the propitious blending of a sturdy Minnesotan and an old-family New Yorker.

Lewis's third novel, *The Job: An American Novel* (1917), presents the symptomatic biography of Una Golden who, first as an "Average Young Woman on a Job" (Lewis's capitals) and later as an unaverage successful entrepreneuse, is one of many "creating a new age" of American business. But after the probing cultural analysis of *The Job* came the self-indulgent interlude of *The Innocents* (1917), a sentimental tale of an old couple who sink to trampdom only to rise to the glories of small-town respectability.

In *Free Air* (1919) Lewis presumably meant to return to his efforts at a comprehensive American realism. The everyman-hero, Milt Daggett, is a self-employed mechanic, inventive and sensibly ambitious. Like Carl Ericson, he is a version of the "American Adam" figure in his independence, his freedom from encumbering tradition, his determination to make a better life on whatever "frontiers" of adventure may be available in his time. And again, Lewis contrives a symbolic marriage of the self-reliant Midwesterner to a wealthy Easterner. But the courtship of these two "playmates" is really much more sentimental than symbolic. Although the patches of sociological illustration in *Free Air* are reasonably strong, the old thin spots in Lewis's fictional fabric have worn through.

In all of his first five novels he had been torn between his intellectual desire for social realism and his emotional proclivity for "romance"— meaning adventure out of the ordinary, implying glamour, and often entailing (though certainly Lewis did not deliberately choose that it should) schoolboy sentimentalism. It was not impossible for these two tendencies to be reconciled, but he had not yet succeeded in reconciling them, because the romantic side of his nature kept subduing the sceptical side. Doubtless he could have kept on in the same vein and continued to make a nice living. There were highly literate readers, however, who would not be content if he failed to progress beyond the promise he had shown. Nor would Lewis himself. He could not contentedly rest on the laurels he had got for a good ear, the keen eye of an historian, and the ability to project himself into the lives of his protagonists with uncommon understanding.

The question was, could he face up to the duality of his interests and make that previous weakness his greatest strength? The answer was *Main Street* (1920), which came upon the American reading public like a tornado out of the Middle West. At the time, it may have appeared to represent an about-face in Lewis's professional attitude. From the celebration of national potentialities he had turned to the castigation of national failings, from social commentary to social criticism. This was not a total about-face; it was a shift in emphasis. In the early stories Lewis had tried to show deficiencies as well as virtues in the national character. With *Main Street,* and thereafter, the emphasis fell more heavily on the deficiencies, for Lewis had decided that these needed more attention than the progress and expectations that virtually everyone now seemed contented with. But the criticism in his best fiction is not simple denigration or iconoclasm: it represents the optimist's disappointment at finding his hopes forestalled, and it still reflects, even in the satiric venom of *Elmer Gantry,* the humanity of outlook that had generated the initial optimism.

Though this is essentially the case with Carol Kennicott's disenchantment in her attempts to improve the world of Gopher Prairie, those who identified Carol with her creator oversimplified the texture of *Main Street.* Carol is often foolish. The means she chooses to serve her admirable ends are usually rash or naive, and she herself comes finally, although somewhat imperfectly, to recognize her own shortcomings when she returns to Will a wiser wife, with more realistic hopes for making the best of a world that leaves much to be desired. Will Kennicott, by no means an unsympathetic character, represents another aspect of Lewis's own nature. His more earthy values may not be so poignantly accented as Carol's thwarted dreams of a cultured community, but they are not to be sneered at. Lewis had at last recognized his emotional-intellectual ambivalences and molded the recognition into a first-rate novel. Or, to put the matter in slightly different terms, Carol does represent the author's self, but it is a self observed and honestly depicted.

Within the decade inaugurated by the thoroughgoing success of *Main Street* and capped by his acceptance of the Nobel Prize, Lewis published also *Babbitt* (1922), *Arrowsmith* (1925), *Elmer Gantry* (1927), and *Dodsworth* (1929). The fact that the period included the lesser *Mantrap* (1926) and *The Man Who Knew Coolidge* (1928) can hardly prevent our judging it a brilliant decade. The dissimilarities among the five best novels suggest not the old indecision, but acquired versatility.

The very different *Babbitt* followed *Main Street,* and with no less success. Its critical reception was deservedly enthusiastic, for it is really a better novel than its predecessor. Where *Main Street* had signalled a necessary revolt against the ingrown values of the village, *Babbitt* demonstrated that these values prevailed in cities as well as country towns. With the possible exception of its "loose" structure, *Babbitt* shows Lewis doing best the things that he could do well. His reportorial eye was so keen that his description of mores, fads and fashions, indicative physical surroundings and the minutiae of daily life could serve as a time capsule buried to satisfy the curiosity of future centuries. We see the inside and outside of the Babbitts' house with excruciating clarity, and a deceptively simple list of the items in Babbitt's pocket reveals his way of life, his system of values. Like many of Lewis's protagonists, George Babbitt is a carefully, instrumentally distorted version of Lewis's self. He is a well-meaning, clubbable, but far from perfect man, internally torn between a troubled, barely understood craving for romance or spiritual nourishment and the ever impinging demands of pragmatic reality: there he lies on his sleeping-porch, teetering helplessly between his escapist dream and the commanding call of his expensive, mass-produced alarm clock. It was a special gift of Lewis's to reveal without fanfare the secret, inchoate life within—the thin dreamer struggling to get out of the fat conformist that encases him. Lewis knew that no Babbitt is all Babbittry, and that is why his major types are never merely types. *Babbitt* contains other varieties of Lewisean excellence: the hilarious spates of plain-folks "booster" talk, the sharply perceived submission to the ineffable potency of status symbols, the "reported" dialogue which, without apparent pointing or authorial comment, convicts the speaker of the crime he denies ("Now, I haven't got one particle of race-prejudice"), the forcible descriptive rhetoric of droning repetition which indicates that Lewis's is fundamentally an oral or tall-story form of humor—all those inventions and devices that enabled him to illustrate with unrivalled effectiveness the American life of not quiet, but noisy desperation.

After *Babbitt* came the very different *Arrowsmith*, a relatively heroic novel about a man with real ability and a real faith, who manages finally to escape the world of foolish, futile dreams and fancy alarm clocks. But before we consider the theme and structure of *Arrowsmith*, a glimpse of Lewis's other novels of the twenties may give us a clearer idea of its place in the framework of his career. *Arrowsmith* was, to no one's great delight, followed by a protracted slick-magazine adventure story. *Mantrap* is an example of the prolific writer's peril, the lapse that has value only as it sheds auxiliary light on his genuine achievements. The writing of it may be considered a testing and partly a purging action, insofar as Lewis appears to have tried to perfect or get rid of such old thematic devices as the ameliorative retreat to the wilderness (the native American form of pastoral romance) and the conjoining of contraries both in friendship and in marriage, by bringing them baldly to the fore in this book. In retrospect, *Mantrap* looks like a makeshift way-station between *Arrowsmith* and *Elmer Gantry*, two remarkably dissimilar novels.

Bernard De Voto has argued that Lewis was not a realist but a satirist, a former radical optimist gone sour and lashing out. Applied to the whole of Lewis's work, this judgment has an element of truth in it; it is just wrong enough to be a bum steer. But it applies with adequate precision to *Elmer Gantry*. Lacking the subtlety and involution of Swift's best work, *Elmer Gantry* is Lewis's most "Swiftian" novel in the sense that it is primarily and relentlessly satiric. The title character is a villain, a ruthless self-serving preacher with none of the saving graces or extenuating circumstances that warrant some sympathy for each of the other protagonists (except Lowell Schmaltz, and the relatively harmless Schmaltz is not so much a protagonist as a device). Elmer Gantry is a vital character. If we abstract a list of all his traits and deeds, we may think him melodramatically incredible; yet in the experience of reading the novel we cannot, much as we would like to, deny that he is powerfully alive, full of drive and animal cunning, capable of forceful influence, and very frightening.

If *Mantrap* served as a necessary preparation for the asperity of *Elmer Gantry* by allowing the author to straighten out some of the kinks in his sentimental preferences, *The Man Who Knew Coolidge* may have helped to clear the way for *Dodsworth,* venting the Lewis spleen at numerous forms of American humbug. *The Man Who Knew Coolidge* is a minor *tour de force,* remarkable for the author's ability to caricature a type by no other means than mimicry of speech. But the book as a whole is too much. In his six exterior monologues the long-windedness of "Lowell Schmaltz, Constructive and Nordic Citizen" becomes as wearing to read as it would be to hear in real life. The book is worth pausing over just long enough to remark that Schmaltz differs from Lewis's more successful principal characters in being all surface and endless gab, ultimately a mere gimmick of satiric illustration.

In *Dodsworth,* the mellowest of the major works, the hero is as sympathetic—though not so potentially significant—a character as Arrowsmith; and the portrayal of him is seldom if ever distorted by a diversionary jab at phenomena of no special relevance to the progress of the plot. Of course sociological reflections arise, and as with other of Lewis's heroes, it is possible to read Dodsworth's story as prototypal. But the sociological elements neither insist on primacy nor take the form of obtrusive jeremiads. Oddly enough, a predecessor that *Dodsworth* calls to mind is Henry James. The novel has a kind of Jamesean quietness, an unhurried way of proceeding, and a confident forbearance of pointing morals.

Readers who thought at the time that the mellowness of *Dodsworth* signified a settling down of Lewis's writing should have known better. Typically, he took up a whole new area of interest in *Ann Vickers* (1933): the conditions and management of prisons. Sex is treated more openly than in previous novels (in *Elmer Gantry* it had necessarily been treated more brutally). A few reviewers thought this first post-Nobel novel showed a real advance, a further maturing of Lewis's abilities. Nowadays, scarcely anyone would maintain that the later works come up to the quality of the five novels that earned him the Prize. In any case, he stuck to his task of anatomizing the nation: the long promised labor novel never appeared, but he did turn out a hotel novel, an anti-fascist novel, a theater novel, a novel—as always, in the vanguard, before it became voguish to treat the issue—on the "racial question," and so forth.

Lewis had begun to publish at a time when every writer dreamed of producing The Great American Novel. It was a mad dream. However surprisingly close a Dos Passos or a Fitzgerald may have come to creating *A* Great American Novel, and however gamely Lewis himself may have sometimes courted the vision, he had sense enough to see the madness of dreaming that one book could encompass all that welter of diversity; so he tried instead to write a great American set of novels. And he did; at any rate, well enough to merit comparison with Balzac. If the totality of Lewis's writing falls short of being a definitive human comedy, it does add up to a significant American comedy.

Thus the specific historical context of *Arrowsmith*. The story of the making of the novel and the impression it made when first published are adequately covered in the reviews and analyses collected in this anthology. Its structure, as these commentaries indicate, requires no elaborate parsing. The course of the story unfolds in strict chronological order as effect inevitably follows cause, without conspicuous digression or flashback. The plot is "episodic," in the sense that a great deal of ground is covered and one set of events may follow another without full demonstration of inevitability in the sequence. But this does not mean that the nature of causation is simplistic: there is the force of cultural heritage, in the venturing spirit that Martin has inherited from the pioneers of the opening section; there is the influence of such early experience as his pre-apprenticeship in the scruffy office of Doc Vickerson; then there is that element which determines whether or to what extent the factors of inheritance, environment, experience and training will have force,—the element of individual character (one has to assume that Martin and Angus Duer, for example, would be markedly different no matter how similar their backgrounds and upbringings); and in Martin's dedication to the sanctity of quantifiable truth, there is a sort of "final cause," the dream or ultimate goal for which he is willing to struggle and sacrifice. This complexity of implied causation precludes our calling *Arrowsmith* a "naturalistic" novel; personal limitations and external obstacles notwithstanding, Martin does have choice and is able to overcome.

To the outward eye, then, *Arrowsmith* is a structurally uncomplicated fictional biography. It is "realistic" in its avoidance of fantasy and supernatural intervention, in its adherence to the laws of commonsense probability, in its credibilizing accumulation of mundane detail, and not least in the mottled character of its hero. If the narrative form in which his career is depicted lacks notable complication, the career certainly has its ups and downs, owing as much to the difficulties of man-against-himself as to those of man-against-society. He may be a character without great complexity, in the sense of intellectual breadth or deep philosophical self-questioning—Lewis was not the writer to create a modern Hamlet or Faust—but his life story is by no means a simple romance. And although he undergoes no major change of character—once the elements of that character are clearly established—he does develop as he moves from place to place and from one branch of medical science to another, learning what he must do—and what he must do without—in order to be faithful to his chosen destiny. When Lewis says that Martin is "in no degree a hero," he refers primarily to the fact that this man who has unusual ability and a quester's vision has also his share of human imperfections. His falterings are often of his own making, and when he botches the chance to make a definitive test of the value of his bacteriophage, the cause is his own choice made on the basis of humane emotional considerations instead of the purely intellectual integrity he had hoped to attain—Lewis carefully declines to treat the issues as if they were easy to resolve. Moreover, though Martin undergoes such serious pathos as the death of Leora, the obstacles that thwart him are often petty almost to the point of being ridiculous, as if to say that straitened American idealism cannot claim even so much as significantly tragic circumstances.

This consideration, however, takes us out of the realm of strictly personal history. *Arrowsmith* has plenty of minor characters, many of whom Lewis has fairly adroitly woven into the narrative. One thinks, for instance, of the reappearance of Irve Watters in Nautilus, Ira Hinkley on the plague-stricken island, and Clif Clawson in Manhattan, not to mention that old-fashioned where-are-they-now catalogue in the last chapter. Such characters are intended to signify not only as they relate particularly to Martin Arrowsmith, but also as they reveal varying aspects of American society. Lewis offers a full spectrum of men of science: each of the students and faculty members at medical school, and each doctor and researcher met later, represents a type.

A large part of the novel's impressiveness stems from the way it functions throughout on two distinct though effectively interrelated levels, the personal and the social. It is on the social level, of course, that the matter of theme becomes of prime import in analysis of *Arrowsmith*; the danger is that in abstracting a message from one level of narrative significance we may easily omit qualifications implied by the other level. There is nothing wrong with interpreting Martin's experience as representative of the fate of idealism or the disinterested search for truth in twentieth-century America, so long as we remember that the idealism has its dubious aspects and that questions are raised about the validity of his disinterest. To read the novel as simply an attack on contemporary mores, using a saintly victim for its weapon, is to do Lewis and ourselves the disservice of careless reading. *Arrowsmith* may stand as proof that a book which seems to present no fascinating difficulties of intellectual density, structural involution, or subtle irony, nevertheless needs to be read with constant attention to nuance and the complication of, say, one value impinging on another. At bottom what the novel "says" is nothing less than all that is said, thought, done, and intimated in the fictive reality that it brings to life.

The crucial question of criticism may be whether *Arrowsmith* is fully alive, forever struggling to be born, or now dead from aging. But this is a question that can properly be put only when we have resolved to try the novel on its own grounds, according to the laws of form and meaning that it implicitly ratifies. Is the background material provided in the first chapter meaningfully developed or implicated in the course of the narrative (in the treatment of a latter-day pioneer spirit and, e.g., in the suggested parallel between Doc Vickerson's and Gottlieb's influence on Martin)? Is the recurrent motif of science as a religion (outlined in the excerpt from D. J. Dooley's book) adequately integrated with other features in the portrayal of Martin's career? Is the, so to speak, semi-subplot of Gottlieb's experience in America serviceable as a foil to highlight Martin's story? Is Leora's death in St. Hubert a mere convenience of plot, enabling Lewis to intensify Martin's island crisis and later to associate him with a different stratum of society, or is it carefully worked into the cumulative complex of events (e.g., with regard to what we have learned of her personal habits, their relationship, and the fact that she dies from the very thing he has devised to save human lives)? Is Martin himself—as Lewis represents him—meant to be admired, sympathized with, puzzled over, or deplored for his final retreat into pastoral monasticism? Is the quality of American life shown in the novel now pertinent to an understanding of the world we live in? These are a few of the diverse issues that thorough analysis must attend to.

Questions of characterization and genre, like those of thematic meaning and integrity of plot, are best approached with reference to the book's overall doubleness. "Novel" or "satire"? Both; not now one and now the other, but simultaneously both. *Arrowsmith* is a novel because, from first to last, it dramatizes the experience of an individual, grappling in effect with the immemorial puzzle of who am I and what should I do. It is a satire because, no less pervasively, it criticizes the obstructive components of this individual's society by means of humorous and discomforting distortion. There is nothing singular about this simultaneity: it belongs to a tradition dignified by such names as Fielding, Dickens, Butler, and Twain.

As for characterization, the general truth is that only a few characters are fully realized; the rest are simplified types or caricatures (though that seems too restrictive a term for such a lively type as Pickerbaugh). The former, quite obviously, are those whose lives have intrinsic meaning on the personal level, and the caricatures matter primarily—if not exclusively—by virtue of their extrinsic reference. Even the most rounded of Lewis's characters are likely to have suggestive names, and in some cases—Rippleton Holabird?—this technique of emphasis may become oppressive. Still, Lewis could create characters who seem real in their three-dimensionality, and when these persons can convincingly co-exist with the one-sided types—that is, when an Arrowsmith and a Pickerbaugh do not appear to belong to quite separate fictional worlds—their creator deserves credit for a feat of art. Leora has been perhaps too lavishly praised; she is indeed a likeable lady, and much more convincing than the second Mrs. Arrowsmith, but she no longer seems on a par with the characters of Jane Austen. The portrayal of Gottlieb, on the other hand, deserves more careful examination. He is not so perfectly heroic as some discussions of the novel imply: we know that he has been more or less a failure as a father, that he is often foolishly impractical and temperamental in his professional conduct and, most pathetically, that he lets pride triumph over good sense when he accepts the directorship at McGurk Institute. And we know him with surprising fullness, considering how remote a person he is and how economically the information is conveyed—his biographical background, his physical appearance, his speech, his attitudes and tastes, his blunders and tribulations, finally his lifeless last days.

The point of view of *Arrowsmith* is at once simple and problematical. The novel is written from a vantage of authorial omniscience, with a good deal of authorial commentary telling us rather than dramatizing what a character feels or thinks, yet with little authorial "intrusion" in the form of abstract statement lacking dramatic illustration. Though the narrative is in the third person, most often the focus is on what Martin says and does or on what he could reasonably be expected to know about. The major divergences from this focus come at the very first and last, where a greater narrative distance is used to help define the broader contexts of Martin's history. Point of view becomes problematical when we turn to the aesthetic consideration of the narrative's literary texture: the character of the prose and tone. Not that the prose style is inappropriate. The problem is that it seems at times all too accidentally appropriate. Could Lewis have intended that some of the more "poetic" passages of description should accurately reflect the uncultivated side of Martin's intellect by being sophomorically purple? Benefit of doubt might be given to those passages that indirectly represent Martin's personal reactions, but when we examine the "fine writing" that lacks this alibi—and when we look to other Lewis novels for corroboration—we have to conclude that the novelist is at fault. With respect to tone as implied in the evaluation of persons and events, we have no difficulty deciding what in general is presented satirically and what sympathetically, but it is not always easy to tell exactly how we are meant to react. What are we to make of Lewis's insistence that Martin and Joyce look so "utterly alike" that they could be taken for twins? Is Martin's minimal concern for his son meant to dampen respect for his decision to forgo the comforts of high life? Is Sondelius—whom Lewis once called his favorite character—made so unusually attractive in order that his zealous, humanitarian practicalism should weigh against the excessive purity of Gottlieb's approach to science?

While admiring Lewis for his fundamental reality principle, his refusal to blink the complexity of issues—like Martin's conduct in St. Hubert—that could have been treated with dishonest simplicity, we should acknowledge that some of the critics' disagreements may result not from superficial analysis, but from unintentional ambiguity or obscurity in the novel. The very fact that *Arrowsmith* is a good novel warrants careful scrutiny both of the novel itself and of what has been written about it.

\*     \*     \*

The selections of criticism gathered here include the best that has been written on *Arrowsmith* and are as representative of the range of opinion as could be—short of reprinting righteously intemperate reviews by doctors who had nothing to say of the book as a novel, or later commentary that is either extremely inaccurate or dull.\* Omission of Continental criticism does not mean a lack of concern with Lewis abroad. The Nobel Prize is not given to writers unknown or unrespected in Europe. Carl L. Anderson's book on *The Swedish Acceptance of American Literature* naturally centers on the critical reception of our first Nobel laureate, but Swedish criticism, like the German and French, adds little or nothing to what has been said in England and America. Even in Italian journals, where Lewis is now enjoying something of a revival, the essays published so far shed no

---

\* In order to include all the more important or interesting articles and excerpts from books, it has been necessary to make certain cuts in some of the longer ones and to delete virtually all the original footnotes. The selections by Sherman, Richardson, Ober, Dooley, Van Doren, Mencken, Lovett, and Canby are thus reprinted in somewhat shortened form, and four commentaries—by Richardson, Rosenberg, Dooley, and Grebstein—are reprinted without their scholarly apparatus. In all cases I have tried to preserve the main points as well as the conclusions of the critics' arguments.

special light on *Arrowsmith*. In other words, the few selections from
English periodicals are reasonably typical of all European criticism.
"Why Sinclair Lewis Got the Nobel Prize," the official address by
Karlfeldt, the Permanent Secretary of the Swedish Academy, has been
included because it states concisely the international assessment of
Lewis when he was at the peak of his powers. Only the selection by
Carl Van Doren, one of Lewis's most sympathetic critics, attempts an
overview of the novelist's entire career in the light of a significant
development in twentieth-century American letters. Other evaluations
of the whole of Lewis's work can be found in Mark Schorer's *Sinclair
Lewis* in the companion Twentieth Century Views series, especially
the fine essays by Whipple, Kazin, Lippmann, and Mumford; and in
the books by Schorer, Grebstein, and Dooley listed in the bibliography
of the present volume.

Over half of the selections reprinted here are reviews, for the simple
reason that this imbalance reflects the course of Lewis's reputation.
By the end of the twenties, he was regarded as the nation's leading
novelist. In the thirties, when new issues and new standards of literary
judgment came to the fore, he began to sink into the background.
Critics who had initially praised him—perhaps too warmly—began to
retract with a vehemence that suggested personal embarrassment.
Bernard De Voto, for instance, who had reviewed *Arrowsmith* with a
Thesaurus-like series of superlatives, later condemned the book as
"romantic, sentimental, and above all trivial." Apparently it was no
longer fashionable, because it was no longer so necessary, to castigate
smug prejudice, cultural inertia, and materialistic standardization; a
"religion" of pure science, moreover, was bound to look dated once its
mysteries became more accessible to common knowledge. The general
public—partly, ironically, owing to Lewis's own insistent proddings—
had become more sophisticated. And professional criticism had become
a more refined exercise, most often interpreted to exclude the likes
of Lewis as insufficiently "literary." He had not the exquisite aesthetic
sensibility of Henry James, or (to cite other Nobel laureates) the
recondite intellectuality of T. S. Eliot, or O'Neill's experimental interest in form, or Faulkner's infectious compulsion to grope through
metaphysical thickets. Not much of a stylist and not extraordinarily
profound, Lewis has been judged to be important primarily as an
historical phenomenon. Perhaps we should be willing to concede an
argument over labeling; we might, that is, hold on to Lewis's total
achievement as something other than literary, while acknowledging
that *Arrowsmith* and his other best works can still please us and test
us and instruct us in ways not exclusively sociological. In the past few
years, at any rate, there are signs that the tide may again be turning
in Lewis's favor: since 1960, there have appeared new paperback

editions of several of the novels; a monumental biography by one of the most sensitive critics of our time; Schorer's collection of Twentieth Century Views; a very solid critical analysis as part of a series on "United States Authors"; several essays, including two on *Arrowsmith* reprinted here; and most recently, an independent study which purports to focus on the *art* of Sinclair Lewis. D. J. Dooley says that his *Art of Sinclair Lewis* is not meant to be exhaustive; he intends it, rather, to be "a contribution to the continuing debate over his place in American letters." The issues, evidently, are again open to serious debate. And the greatest value of the following commentaries may consist not so much in what is said about *Arrowsmith*—though much is said well—as in the room they leave for saying more.

## PART ONE

*Interpretations*

# A Way Out: Sinclair Lewis Discovers a Hero

## *by Stuart P. Sherman*

I came to Mr. Lewis's new novel with a kind of anxious expectation. Two years ago, when from his swift aircraft he was bombarding
Zenith, I reviewed his work up to that point and set forth reasons
for believing him "capable of fresh flights for distance and altitude."
Incidentally, I occasioned wrath in celestial minds by speaking of
his "significance." Mrs. Mary Colum tells me that I have no literary
principles and that Mr. Lewis has no literary significance. Mr. Ernest
Boyd tells me that I have principles, but that a person of my principles has no right to perceive Mr. Lewis's significance. This is confusing. Since I am about to pain both of these conscientious critics
by praising Mr. Lewis again, I had better repeat some of my reasons
for maintaining that, though he is disgracefully popular, he is a
sound artist and belongs "inside literature."

Fire from heaven and graces "beyond the reach of art" commonplace minds perhaps should not meddle with, but concerning these
words "art" and "artist" celestial minds are becoming needlessly
mystical and finical. I feel a mundane unwillingness to have these
words taken away from the laity and reserved for sacrosanct uses.
The most indicative sign, not of a celestial mind but of an artist, is
that he knows what to do and how to do it. In his last three novels
Mr. Lewis is a satirist, which is a kind of literary marksman, and his
means seek his ends like bullets. It seems necessary to explain to
celestial minds that, in satire, to hit the mark is *art*.

Among other qualities and faculties of Mr. Lewis's which are useful
in literature I spoke of the velocity of his intelligence; the justice
of his antipathies; a timeliness—part of "the open-eyed efficiency of
genius"—which results from energetic study of himself and his age;
his comprehensive and mordant notation of detail, in unusual combination with a generalizing faculty and a sense for the significant and

*"A Way Out: Sinclair Lewis Discovers a Hero" by Stuart P. Sherman. From*
Books, *the review of* The New York Herald Tribune, *March 8, 1925, pp. 1-2.*
*Ellipses indicate the omission of material from the original text.*

representative aspects of character and social life; and, finally, of
the objectivity of his imagination, which enables him to penetrate
and construct freely, outside the territory of the lyrical and autobiographical "fictionist."

These traits were obvious enough in "Main Street" and "Babbitt,"
but many of the critics did not recognize them. Long accustomed to
a novel which is essentially autobiographical revery, they could not
easily reconcile themselves to a form based upon observation and
constructed by an active, intelligent, critical imagination. There
was too much *mind* in it for art, as they understood art, and so
they called it journalism!

In despite of celestial-minded critics and Pulitzer Prizes, "Main
Street" and "Babbitt" established Mr. Lewis as incomparably our
most stimulating social satirist. Since Charles Dickens lashed us in
"Martin Chuzzlewit" and "American Notes" no other novelist, English or American, has given us a satirical castigation so thorough or
so deserved. "Main Street" and "Babbitt" raised the question whether
Mr. Lewis was anything but a satirist, rudely blurting out his bore-
dom at the humdrum and vulgarity of our great heroic middle class—
a humdrum and a vulgarity which many people consider it the part
of good citizenship to accept and silently to endure as in the order
of nature. These books provoked the trodden worm to such resentful writhings as this: "So he goes on, until his world is one vast
nauseous Pullman smoker full of Rotarians, Fraternians, Boomers,
Realtors and Baboons, getting off one damn fool thing after another."

The indictment is not just; open eyes caught glints of natural
beauty and human worth in Gopher Prairie and Zenith. But it was
in the less familiar novels—in "The Trail of the Hawk," "The Job"
and "Free Air"—that, previous to the appearance of "Arrowsmith,"
one was most made aware that Mr. Lewis is a good lover as well as
a good hater. It was in reading these tales that I first remarked his
passion for persons edged with purpose, for all things clean, supple,
active and darting—"the swoop of the hawk, arrows that go straight
to the mark." Sooner or later, I surmised, his faculty of admiration
would crave release and exercise, and then we should have a new
sort of book to talk about.

I opened "Arrowsmith," as I have said, with grave anxiety, but I
read it with immense satisfaction, sitting back in my chair from time
to time, and wondering, happily, to which pit of journalism celestial-
minded critics would now consign its author. It does mark a new
flight for distance and altitude. It is winged with derision on one
side, but with admiration on the other. It is a book with a butt, but
it is also a book with a hero, with several heroes, and it is a far better
book than "Babbitt." Before I say anything more about that I request

permission to depose that I am not under any oath of obligation to applaud each of Mr. Lewis's novels more loudly than the last.

"Main Street" immediately captivated me with the rich, pungent odor of new tilled soil, with the Hogarthian vigor of its caricatures, its exuberance of comic perception. But "Babbitt," which the general cry of reviewers hailed as superior to its predecessor, I thought less intensely and vividly conceived than "Main Street"—the character drawing less sharp and memorable, the entire social picture inadequately lighted.

"Main Street" had, in the way of material civilization, led to Zenith. But where should we go from there? To New York? Mr. Lewis did not even suggest New York—though of course it is the Mahomet's Paradise at the end of "Main Street." He rang down the curtain, leaving us with a sense that nothing was to be gained by going anywhere from Zenith—in any of the directions toward which its inhabitants were headed.

Now, the sense that life must be lived but that life is not, in any direction, worth while is a futile sense. It is not worth talking about. No great work of art with which I am acquainted communicates as the ultimate gist of its message the sense of futility. Even a beautiful and *ineffectual* angel beating *in the void its* luminous wings *in vain* has at least been beautiful and luminous. But Mr. George F. Babbitt's wings were neither luminous nor beautiful, and he was ineffectual. All that prevents Mr. Babbitt from being utterly depressing is his restlessness. That is something, but not much.

A social historian who planned an American *comédie humaine*—a social historian whose intelligence moved at the ordinary tempo, would obviously have attempted in his next book to enter the territory of Mrs. Wharton. Perhaps Mr. Lewis has not adequately observed that territory. I do not know. There are several chapters in the latter part of "Arrowsmith" which suggest that he has glanced into it but that he grew tired of its futility before he got there, and was unwilling, even for the duration of one novel, to seem seeking a way out of the humdrum and vacuity of American life through the inanities of our fashionable "leisure class."

At any rate, in "Arrowsmith" Mr. Lewis turns from the small town and the big town, which he has treated, and from "Society," which he has not treated, to a profession which runs through all the social strata; he turns his satire upon the medical profession and upon institutions for scientific research. The titular hero's career takes him from the bottom to the top. . . .

The book is long but the narrative is not prolix. It goes straight, hard and fast from the opening paragraph to the last, with the earnest fullness of a writer who is dealing with a superabundance of very rich material, yet with marvelous syncopations and abridgments, and in a style of almost telegraphic succinctness. Each of its eight or nine scenes is firmly constituted, impregnated with its proper colors and odors, peopled with the men and women appropriate to it, busy with the talk, action and passion that belong to it.

The language employed by the characters is that used in the United States of America. The medical students and the professors; the rival country doctors; the Nautilus board of health and its political friends and enemies and their wives; the suave money-making Chicago surgeons; the McGurk Institute, with its inter-departmental jealousies, its fussy, pompous director, and the ladies of means and social position who peep in on the experiments and patronize the experimenters and occasionally carry off a promising one in a limousine and marry him--each of these groups authentically buzzes and hums and fusses about one of the scenes of Martin's labors, using its own highly flavored lingo, ranging from medical college slang through the Walt Whitman poetry of the Nautilus board of health to the elaborate technicalities of bacteriological research.

I suppose there is more science and scientific talk in "Arrowsmith" than in any other novel that has hitherto appeared in the world. Some persons, I hear, think there is more than the populace will stand. I think not. Consider those feelers of the public pulse, the newspapers; consider their radio sections. Science as Mr. Lewis handles it is hot with the latest master-passion of this age. He himself is the son of a country doctor, and some of his medical knowledge came to him with his bread and milk. He accounts for his bacteriological lore in a dedication to Dr. Paul H. De Kruif,* his companion on the cruise in which he acquired his West Indian isle. With all explanations made, the amount of his special information is astonishing. Still more astonishing, the special information nowhere clutters the story: it is all at work.

In mentioning the stages of Martin's career I have not told his story. I have merely indicated the scenes. For Martin is not ordinarily ambitious, not a social climber, not even an academic climber. The distinction of his story lies in this, that from point to point he is struggling only for an opportunity to do honest scientific work. Like his friends Gottlieb, Sondelius and Wickett, he is one of the rare men in whom the love of discovering and verifying truth becomes sweeter than wife or child or friend or home or ease or food or sleep or public applause or anything that wealth or societies for

---

* Not precisely a dedication but an acknowledgment in which Lewis recorded his indebtedness to De Kruif "not only for most of the bacteriological and medical material in this tale but equally for his help in the planning of the fable itself." [R.J.G.]

conferring honor can give him. Except scientific curiosity there is nothing especially noble in Martin. Occasionally he is drunk for days together, occasionally he looks at a girl who should not interest him, occasionally he bestirs himself to be nice to his wife. But these are incidents. From first to last he is an essentially single-hearted servant of his mastering scientific passion. In that he finds peace. Or in that he would find peace, so he thinks, if anywhere from the bottom to the top of his career he could discover a nook in his profession, a niche in society, where the pure disinterested pursuit of truth is respected, encouraged or even left undisturbed.

I suppose valiant and angry penmen will rise to accuse Mr. Lewis of gross injustice and libelous caricature in showing up the medical colleges, the medical profession and the institutions for research. For my part, I was surprised at his moderation when I began to consider the number of shocking and true "revelations" which he might have made but did not make. His account of the obstacles encountered by Martin is not sensational. There is nothing in this book of the fanatical and inflammatory "muckraker" or scandalmonger. The sum of his satire consists in the suggestion that the advancement of science, though much prated about in America, is a long way from being the first interest in the quarters of its professed friends. The average doctor, the average teacher, the average researcher, such is Martin's discovery, is not burning with "a hard, gem-like flame," but with a very dull, smoky flame, fanned by pecuniary need, pecuniary greed, humanitarian sympathy, social fear, social aspiration and lust for applause and publicity. . . .

Babbittry with the grave bedside manner of Medicine; Babbitry with the austere uplifted countenance of Science.

It is not a jot worse there than anywhere else—in art, or letters, for example. The satire cuts into the quick of human nature.

There is only one way out. It runs through fire. If there is fire enough within, that doesn't matter.

"Arrowsmith" is hot with the authentic fire in which art and science are purified.

# *Arrowsmith:* Genesis, Development, Versions

## *by Lyon N. Richardson*

Sinclair Lewis wrote into *Arrowsmith* so much of his basic personality that the novel is central to the revelation of the man and his work. Fortunately there is much material at hand pertaining to the genesis of the book; and the opportunity to trace the development of the characters and especially to note a multitude of editorial revisions and the reconstitution of sectional terminations was greatly expanded when, in the midst of his work, Lewis revised the still uncompleted book-manuscript for initial publication as a serial in the *Designer and the Woman's Magazine* from June, 1924, through April, 1925. The editors of the *Designer* also excised a great many passages throughout the manuscript; thus a study of editorial policy may easily be made.

Both Lewis and Paul Henry de Kruif have written of the dramatic origin of *Arrowsmith*.* They had first met in the summer of 1922 "in the office of Dr. Morris Fishbein, of the *Journal of the American Medical Association*," and that evening, during an ardent discussion on medical education, Lewis declared his resolution to write a story of a doctor who, "starting out as a competent general practitioner, emerges as a real scientist, despising ordinary 'success.' " Dr. de Kruif, bacteriologist, fresh from the laboratories of the Rockefeller Institute for Medical Research, agreed to help him. Together they "wandered from Barbados to Panama to Europe; . . . spent hours in laboratories in Panama, in London, in Paris," and "got in five to seven hours of work daily." Lewis typed, with "maps, books, diagrams and paper

---

"*Arrowsmith: Genesis, Development, Versions*" by *Lyon N. Richardson. From* American Literature, *XXVII (May, 1955), 225-244. Copyright © 1955 by Duke University Press. Reprinted by permission of the author and the publisher. Details of evidence presented in support of the conclusions reprinted here have been omitted. Considerations of space have led also to the omission of all but the first of Richardson's 22 footnotes.*

* For quotations in this paragraph, see "Sinclair Lewis at Work," by Lewis, and "An Intimate Glimpse of a Great American Novel in the Making," by Dr. de Kruif, in the *Designer and the Woman's Magazine*, LX, 2, 64 (June, 1924). These are remarks introducing the serialized version. See also "How *Arrowsmith* Was Written," in Barbara G. Spayd, ed., *Arrowsmith* (New York, 1945), pp. xix-xxv.

around him," including Patrick Manson's *Tropical Diseases*; de Kruif instructed him on medical and scientific matters, microbes, and the "lore of laboratories." Especially memorable to de Kruif was the hot Sunday afternoon on San Lucia when they let their imaginations play on a hypothetical sweep of the bubonic plague over the island, which Lewis later developed into a major section of the novel, and he reported that Lewis, "On the surface restless, hasty of temper, genial, . . . is patient, precise and accurate when he sits down to his typewriter." Lewis worked over a year on the novel in London and Fontainebleau.

The Lewis Collection in the Yale University Library contains many maps, diagrams, and notes that Lewis characteristically made to assist him in developing and visualizing a novel. For *Arrowsmith* he created imaginary maps for his Pony River Valley and the town of Wheatsylvania in North Dakota, and for the campus of the medical school of the University of Winnemac, as well as detailed drawings of the first, second, and third floors of the main medical building, the first and second floors of the anatomy building, and the thirtieth floor of the McGurk Building, the two top floors of which housed the McGurk Institute of Biology. Lewis also made a chronology of the life of Martin Arrowsmith and noted a long list of possible titles for the book. Such tentative titles as The Stumbler and The Barbarian clearly indicate certain qualities with which Lewis wished to endow Arrowsmith in "this biography of a young man who was in no degree a hero, who regarded himself as a seeker after truth yet who stumbled and slid back all his life and bogged himself in every obvious morass. . . ." He narrowed the list until the title became Dr. Martin Arrowsmith in the serialized version, and finally simply *Arrowsmith* in the American edition, Lewis noting of Arrowsmith that *"it's his personal and scientific career that counts much more than his medical career."*

In an italicized prefatory note in the book edition of *Arrowsmith,* Lewis generously recognized the service of de Kruif "for his realization of the characters as living people, for his philosophy as a scientist," and for supplying considerable "lore" of laboratories and medical and scientific institutions. In response to a letter of inquiry, Dr. de Kruif has assured the author of this article that part of the origin of Gottlieb—something of his nature and devotion to research—springs from Dr. de Kruif's acquaintance with Dr. Jacques Loeb, who was head of the Division of General Physiology of the Rockefeller Institute, and with Dr. Frederick George Novy, then Professor of Bacteriology and later Dean of the School of Medicine of the University of Michigan, with whom Dr. de Kruif was associated for a decade; further, the McGurk Institute in *Arrowsmith* would not have been so vividly presented if Dr. de Kruif had not been associated recently with the Rockefeller Institute. Yet the principal characters are definitely and chiefly Lewis's creations and partake of his own character.

Arrowsmith is largely a projection of Lewis's own personality. Instinctively Lewis gave the title "The Death of Arrowsmith" to an autobiographical sketch originally published in *Coronet,* July 1, 1941, seventeen years after the publication of the novel in serialized form. And quite seriously in "Self-Portrait" (Berlin, August, 1927), two years after the publication of the book, while it was still a sharply emotional memory, he identified certain of his own aspirations with Max Gottlieb and much of his own "loyalty to love" with Leora Tozer. Lewis here expressed it thus:

> There is really no Sinclair Lewis about whom even that diligent scribbler himself could write, outside of what appears in his characters. All his respect for learning, for integrity, for accuracy, and for the possibilities of human achievement are to be found not in the rather hectic and exaggerative man as his intimates see him, but in his portrait of Professor Max Gottlieb, in *Arrowsmith.* Most of the fellow's capacity for loyalty to love and friendship has gone into Leora in that same novel. . . .

As for Sondelius, Lewis stated in "Self-Portrait" (Nobel Foundation), written in 1930 as an autobiographical sketch for the foundation five years after the book had appeared, that he had made "Gustaf Sondelius, of *Arrowsmith,* a Swede—and to me, Dr. Sondelius is the favorite among all my characters." This elevation of Sondelius to the "favorite" status is of psychological interest, even though it undoubtedly was done on the spur of the moment when Lewis was thinking of his relation to Swedes while writing to the Nobel Foundation. It comes as a bit of a surprise to readers, for Sondelius does not hold a truly prominent place in the novel. Mentioned first on page 171 of the 448-page novel, he does not enter in person until pages 182-185, and he does not appear again until page 336, when Lewis takes time to describe him "as possessing a little of Gottlieb's perception, something of Dad Silva's steady kindliness, something of Terry's tough honesty though none of his scorn of amenities, and with a spicy, dripping richness altogether his own." Thereafter (pp. 338-339) he becomes Arrowsmith's assistant, and Lewis chooses him to accompany Martin and Leora to the island of St. Hubert (pp. 348-350), where he destroys rats and handles official matters relative to the inoculation of the populace during the next twenty-five pages, and dies of the plague (p. 381), sixty-seven pages before the end of the book. Actually, Lewis had drawn Sondelius with the sketchiness of an author creating a puppet of some stature for use in the machinery of a novel, and the character does not become a true creation. Yet Sondelius can be envisioned as possessing most of Gottlieb's integrity without his irascibility, and most of Arrowsmith's devotion to a scientific venture without his somewhat persistent immaturity and lack of balance or ability to be a moderator among men. Thinking of this, Lewis could, on the impulse of the moment, crown Sondelius "the favorite among all my characters," a figure having certain strengths lacking in Arrowsmith and Gottlieb, both of whom more closely partake of Lewis's own personality.

## II

On October 10, 1923, while Lewis was in Europe working on *Arrowsmith*, Alfred Harcourt, his close friend and publisher, in a letter to "Red," reported a telephone call by Sewell Haggard, who told Harcourt that the Butterick people wanted to publish a feature serial during the next year to put the *Designer* "on the map," and he wished to inquire about the availability of a novel he had heard Lewis was finishing. Harcourt replied, "Do you want $50,000 worth?" Thus began a course of negotiations leading to the publication of *Dr. Martin Arrowsmith* in the *Designer*.

Lewis's reply from London on November 6 is significant and characteristic in its insistence that there be no compromise in the nature of the story if it should appear in the *Designer*:

> One thing I wish to emphasize. I suppose Haggard will have to cut, but I will not change the thing into a sunny sweet tale nor will I permit him to. *Does he understand that?* Please let me know, for otherwise he can't have it at any price. (Not that there's much really *offensive* in the novel, anyway. He needn't worry.)

Again from London, on November 12, Lewis reiterated his stand: "As I asked before, does Haggard understand there will be no sunny conventionalities tucked in?"

Lewis's fears proved groundless. Indeed, the arrangement for serial publication was most fortunate in all ways. He received a handsome price from the *Designer*; he enjoyed the extra time given him to develop the book; and, instinctively a journalist, he himself eliminated many scattered short passages which he still felt to be of value in the book but recognized as surplusage in serial form. From London on December 27, 1923, he wrote to Harcourt:

> If I were you (and in this case the you refers to everybody connected with Harcourt-Brace) I don't believe I'd even read the installments that go over to Haggard *because* I am more or less cutting from the book-

manuscript for serial use—cutting out bits of philosophy which will (I think) be of considerable value in the book and little or none in the magazine. Wait till about the end of April, and you'll have the whole book ms. When I come home we can at leisure go over the book ms. and—this will be splendid—I can lay it away for several months and go over the whole thing again just before you start setting, a year or so from now.

The story progressed well. From London, February 9, 1924, he wrote Harcourt that in "about four days" he would be sending another 25,000 words to Haggard, who had cabled regarding the first 40,000 words: "Story splendid"; and on March 4, in another letter to Harcourt, he was sufficiently elated to remark that Haggard had said that "if the whole novel is up to the first 40,000 words, it will be the best thing I have ever done." Actually, Lewis quite realized that different media required different techniques. Not only did he understand the problems of popular journals, for which he had written, but he was thinking of the possibility of a screen version, which Sidney Howard eventually did for a Samuel Goldwyn production, starring Ronald Colman as Arrowsmith and Helen Hayes as Leora, to Lewis's satisfaction; and when Howard adapted *Dodsworth* for the stage, Lewis praised the playwright most enthusiastically, noting that though by reason of the medium the book had been radically changed in detail, the adapter did "preserve, and in the different milieu of the stage sincerely present, the real theme and characters of the story."

The depth of Lewis's interest in the medical and scientific "philosophy" of *Arrowsmith,* his personal willingness to start a controversy, and his faith in advertising are revealed in his letter to Harcourt from Paris, December 27, 1924. *"And,"* he wrote, "besides the individual doctors, the editors of medical journals, the A.M.A. officials, and the college bacteriologists, *have Paul* [de Kruif] make out a list of other scientists to whom it should go in advance"; and he further suggested sending copies to other medical men, "e.g. [Abraham] Flexner," of the Carnegie Foundation for the Advancement of Teaching, who might not like it "quite as much as those who will." No changes in the text in the *Designer* affect Lewis's remarks on science, medicine, or medical institutions and those associated with them.

### III

Scattered throughout the 448 pages of *Arrowsmith* in book form there are 336 complete paragraphs, long and short, not in the *Designer,* and there are at least 103 paragraphs which have been reduced approximately one to three lines and 59 paragraphs which have been cut four to fourteen lines. There are only 26 complete paragraphs unique to the *Designer* and 37 paragraphs to which additions or substitutions were made. It is evident that for purposes of serialization the manuscript was fully and carefully edited without mutilating the fundamental scenes and theme. Indeed, it can well be argued that the story really lost little in the serial form and in many ways was improved by deletions of words and sentences which merely belabored the ideas or were blatant Lewisian expletives and obtrusive, derisive remarks.

Lewis's natural impulse was to be climactic, and *Arrowsmith* is a series of many short, dramatic scenes. Therefore, in spite of the hundreds of textual changes, no structural alterations were necessary to achieve a climax for each installment in the *Designer*; one was always conveniently at hand, at the end of either a chapter or a section within a chapter. Each of the eleven installments closes at a moment of high interest: when Martin goes home "engaged to two girls at once"; when Martin and his bride Leora are separated on their bridal night by her father; when Gottlieb at a crucial moment accepts a position with the McGurk Institute of Biology; when Leora's unborn baby is taken "from her, dead," and she and Martin, "eternally understanding," gaze "in the prairie twilight"; when Leora demands of Martin that he stop flirting with Orchid, and he determines to be successful at Nautilus; when Martin resolves to "make myself succeed" as Director of Public Health at Nautilus; when Martin energetically begins his researches at the McGurk Institute; when it is determined that Martin and Sondelius will go to the Island of St. Hubert; when Martin, "aghast" at his beginning to fall in love with Joyce Lanyon, is "Suddenly . . . out of bed, kneeling, praying to Leora"; when Martin jubilantly resolves to work with Terry at any cost on the action of derivatives of quinine on bacteria; when Martin, resting at evening with Terry in a boat, looks happily forward to further researches in quinine for two or three years, oblivious of home or position. What more in the way of dramatic structure could an editor of a popular journal demand for $50,000?

But though alterations in structure were not necessary, there were many attitudes, ideas, explosions of satirical invective, and uncouth expressions that did need attention and excision. One was the minor problem of expletives. Lewis was opposed to "obscenity" in writing. In "Obscenity and Obscurity" he stated: "I don't like the use, either in a book or in the parlor, the use of any of those Nine Saxon Monosyllables which the sly and the roughneck use to describe natural functions just to be spicy." But expletives such as *damn, hell,* and *by God* were normal with Lewis. He peppered *Arrowsmith* with them whenever he thought Martin (and occasionally some other character)

would use them in moments of passion, exultation, or moral indignation. They were omitted or altered in the *Designer* without loss to the
story; indeed, the story was improved. The reader's general liking and
respect for Martin are enhanced by omissions which actually do not
diminish his impetuosity or convictions.

Nor could the *Designer* find virtue in certain of the remarks of Lewis
rising from his natural satirical bent and his indignation at moral
smugness. These remarks occasionally took the form of mere buzzing
and stinging at random, including the mention of religious affiliations
in a derogatory way. Lewis recognized this limitation of his powers of
precision in expressing his true feeling. In "Self-Portrait" (Berlin,
August, 1927) he wrote: "Why, this man, still so near to being an out
and out Methodist or Lutheran . . . , is so infuriated by ministers
who . . . keep from ever admitting publicly their confusing doubts
that he risks losing all the good friends he once had among the ministers by the denunciations in *Elmer Gantry*," and the strong satirical
strain in him continually cost him friendships throughout his life. He
was essentially lonely.

Throughout *Arrowsmith* there is no favorable response to religious
institutions or to persons affiliated with them; Lewis's sympathy is reserved for only one man with conscientious convictions about religion
—Sondelius, the sincere agnostic. Lewis's remarks in this area are frequently omitted in the *Designer,* and the deletions reveal the distinc-
tions in attitude between him and the editorial principles governing
the magazine. . . .

As a novel mixed with satire and sympathy, *Arrowsmith* is peopled
with characters subjectively drawn for a purpose. They stand as revelations of Lewis's responses toward different types of men. They are
characters whom he despised or admired, creatures endowed either
with characteristics he detested or with energy and ideals and foibles
he could treat sympathetically and with understanding. As Martin
Arrowsmith and Gustaf Sondelius and Max Gottlieb are of his own
blood, they have both virtues and limitations. In contrast to these,
for example, there is Angus Duer, the cool, self-centered valedictorian
medical student who becomes a capable surgeon with an eye to wealth,
and who keeps in good physical trim, allowing himself "only one drink
daily" (p. 279). Lewis somewhat envied Duer's capabilities, yet he
despised him with a hate so deep that he unnecessarily, perhaps un-
believably for the readers, made him mentally a murderer. But in general there is a mixture of strengths and weaknesses in Lewis's characters, though some of the weaknesses occasionally seem to have been
gratuitously bestowed on them by the author rather than being necessarily inherent. The version of *Arrowsmith* in the Designer omits a
number of the grosser attributes. Sometimes the omissions show an

unwarranted regard for the sensibilities of the readers, sometimes the omissions relieve the story of paragraphs which merely belabor issues and impede the flow of the narrative, and sometimes they clear the text of rather unjustifiable satirical angularities. . . .

In his desire to portray Martin Arrowsmith realistically as a young man possessed of rather grave faults, Lewis gave him emotional characteristics which the *Designer* excised; and he also described brief scenes in the relationship of Martin with Madeline Fox, Orchid Pickerbaugh, and his two wives, Leora Tozer and Joyce Lanyon, which the *Designer* removed without harming the theme of the novel. While Martin is paying his attentions to Madeline Fox before his marriage to Leora Tozer, the *Designer* does not allow Martin to be characterized as a young man who, though not a Don Juan, was nevertheless one of whom it could not be said that his "intentions . . . were what is called 'honorable.' . . . He wanted—like most poor and ardent young men in such a case, he wanted all he could get" (p. 44). When Martin and Leora enter her parents' home after the elopement, the readers are not too clearly informed that Mr. Tozer orders his daughter to her own room alone; there is no statement that they "would in no way, uh, act as though they were married till he gave permission," or that, as for Martin, "That was his bridal night; tossing in his bed, ten yards from her" (p. 105). . . .

Lewis's dominant motive in writing *Arrowsmith* was to extol the truly professional spirit in medical teaching and research, and to expose all intruding chicanery, greed, egotism, and ignorance. So as a satirist he and de Kruif endowed the McGurk Institute and some of its men with characteristics he wished to pillory. He struck out boldly, often mockingly, and some of his remarks were excised from the *Designer*. . . .

Certain medical diseases and references are omitted from the *Designer* in deference to the feelings—or the supposed feelings—of its feminine readers. The excision of these items does somewhat weaken the impact of the story, though in a few instances the omissions lighten Lewis's too heavy hand. For example, Lewis overworked references to the Wassermann test in the book, and this test is entirely excised for the *Designer*. During the illness of Leora in pregnancy, Arrowsmith, in the *Designer*, does not denounce "Nature for her way of tricking human beings, by every gay device of moonlight and white limbs and reaching loneliness, into having babies, then making birth as cruel and clumsy and wasteful as she could" (p. 173). And either Lewis or the editor of the *Designer* did not care to publish in the magazine the whole section dealing with Martin's suffering from neurasthenia (pp. 316-319): the readers never learn that for a short time he read subway posters backwards, feared darkness, thought that burglars might be about, felt the "cord of an assassin squeezing his throat," and drifted into anthropophobia and siderodromophobia.

Associated with these passages are a few others excised from the *Designer* as probably being too repulsive for its readers. They are scenes which do add a certain power to the book, but they are strongly grotesque. . . .

The text of the *Designer* lacks a number of facts and also a number of jabs at persons and concepts which any satirist has a right to include, but which are extraneous Lewisian comments not well woven into the fabric of the story. . . .

There are, finally, a number of excisions made solely to shorten the novel for serialization, and the absence of these passages need not be lamented. Typical examples are the description of Loizeau operating at a clinic (pp. 14-15), much of the early life of Gottlieb (pp. 123-125), some of the bustling activities of Arrowsmith at the McGurk Institute while engaged in research (pp. 307-314), certain of the passages elaborating Gottlieb's tribulations as Director of the McGurk Institute (pp. 334-338), a quotation from a scientific paper read by Arrowsmith (p. 406), and the visits of the social set to Martin's laboratory (pp. 435-437).

## IV

The passages that appear in the *Designer* but not in the book are of two types: they are slight alterations inserted to fill lacunae made by the excision of text in the book not appearing in the *Designer,* or they are passages which Lewis may have discarded in the process of revising his manuscript to improve the novel in book form. There are many slight changes, and nine places where one or more paragraphs are to be found only in the *Designer.* . . .

There are many references to alcoholic drinks both in the book and in the *Designer,* and some of the references in the book are not in the magazine; but, oddly enough, there also are some other references in the *Designer* which are not in the book. Only in the *Designer* the chief steward sends up a bottle of Scotch, Sondelius invents "a drink made chiefly of cognac and Grand Marnier," the governor gives Arrowsmith a glass of Napoleon brandy, Sondelius proposes "a drink at the Ice House" and has too many "planter's punches," Terry suggests that Martin come to his room for a drink, Martin and Terry have a drink from "Roger Lanyon's ancestral stock," and Joyce mentions Martin's "many whiskey sodas." Lewis probably recognized that he had overloaded his story with drinks beyond excuse or occasion for them.

Lewis encountered no difficulty in writing of the courtship and married life of Martin and Leora; he breathed life into them. But he could not well portray the prenuptial and nuptial life of Martin and Joyce; he could not bring these scenes fully to life. He must have sensed this failure, for there are three passages in the thirty-seventh chapter which are in the *Designer* but were cut out or revised in the book. . . .

## V

No reader may doubt that three purposes possessed Lewis's mind as he wrote *Arrowsmith*: to give full allegiance to scientists wholly devoted to basic research in medicine, to satirize those in medical research who are not truly dedicated to their profession, and to tell a story of young love as realistically and sympathetically as he could.

The fact that his novels have not retained their full popular impact is to some degree the common fate of works of satirists that bear the date and seal of their generation in aura and manner. To each age its own satirical tone, its impulse to rewrite history. With the passage of time, certain limitations of Lewis's literary skill and the more angular characteristics of his satire become readily discernible. In *Arrowsmith,* emphasis is sought too frequently by the simple device of expletives. Hypocrisy, selfishness, mediocrity, and smallness of mind of persons in colleges, churches, the medical profession, and medical research institutions too frequently are satirized with the petulant impatience of a zealot unarmed by humor. The mature reader is bothered not only by the many climaxes, some of which are artificial, but by the tyranny of the author over his characters. Scorn and ridicule often make visible the strings leading from most of the characters to the manipulating hands of the author.

These limitations are less noticeable in the version edited for the *Designer.* Although the many climaxes that Lewis contrived for his effects are more conspicuous in the *Designer* than in the book, and although the few paragraphs deleted from the *Designer* revisions are to the advantage of the book, most of the many deletions made for the *Designer* removed irritating blemishes. Even the omission of the nonsatirical expository passages lessens our sense of Lewis's domination over his characters; Gottlieb seems the more real when commentary is reduced. Lewis and the editor of the *Designer* improved the story, though the author, in his eagerness to challenge hypocrisy and mediocrity, would not believe it.

# Sinclair Lewis: *Arrowsmith*

## *by T. K. Whipple*

In Arrowsmith, as in Main Street and Babbitt, Sinclair Lewis is interesting chiefly as a social critic, but this has never been his only interest. He is a recorder as well as a critic of society; he is, after all, at least at times, a novelist; and he is the product as well as the critic of the society which he depicts. When I call him the "product" of it, I mean that he has gone through it and willy-nilly has been affected by it. To reproduce American society, to point out its faults, and to illustrate the effect of this society on a writer who grows up in it— this, surely, is to possess significance. Arrowsmith, like its predecessors, has all these elements of interest, but in somewhat different proportions. It pictures and it satirizes American life; its main interest, however, lies in the parallel which it suggests with the author's own life —in that it shows how the American environment affects the creative spirit. Of this theme Sinclair Lewis's whole works may be taken as in a sense illustrations.

Martin Arrowsmith is a physician who becomes a bacteriologist. Before he finally takes refuge in the wilds of Vermont where he can pursue his researches undisturbed, he encounters all the difficulties which the United States puts in the way of a doctor and an investigator who would like to be honest; he struggles with the commercialism of the medical school, the quackery which thrives in the country, the politics and fraud of a Department of Public Health in a small city, the more refined commercialism of a metropolitan clinic, and the social and financial temptations of a great institute for research. He is offered every possible inducement to prostitute himself to an easy success— manifest, worldly success. Nor is he indifferent to the pressures which are brought to bear on him; on the contrary, being a scientist by instinct rather than by reasoned conviction, he wins out in spite of himself. He would like to succeed, he has been contaminated by the success-worship with which he is surrounded, but he is unable to cope

"*Sinclair Lewis:* Arrowsmith" *by T. K. Whipple. From* The New Republic, *XLII (April 15, 1925), Part II, 3-5. Copyright 1925 by* The New Republic. *Reprinted by permission of Mrs. T. K. Whipple.*

with an ineluctable honesty and stubborn drive in himself. In the end he succumbs to his own integrity.

To describe Arrowsmith as an attack on the medical profession is utterly inadequate. It is an attack on the United States. It is the story of any scientist, or any seeker for the truth—chemist, economist, historian, philosopher, theologian. Nor does it differ essentially from the story of the artist, of whatever species. It tells, in short, the troubles and obstacles met by all those who in this practical land of ours prefer, in Aristotle's terms, the theoretic to the active life, or, in equivalent terms, the creative to the acquisitive, or the contemplative to the practical, life. It deals therefore with the most important theme, in my opinion, of all afforded by American life, and with one of the crucial questions of the ages. The quarrel is a persistent one, because it grows from a fundamental opposition between two types of people; the type on the one hand that cares only for getting on—for making good, for succeeding—and the type on the other that cares less for mere personal advancement and more for taking in the experiences of the journey and for asking "Why?" and "Whither?" The former type, the practical, is opposed to all those disinterested activities which disregard the main chance—the pursuit of knowledge and beauty for their own sake, the wish to investigate or to enjoy—which to the second type constitute the reasons for existence. Practical men, one might say, care only to exploit their environment; theoretic or contemplative men care only to get acquainted with it, to explore and realize and experience it as fully as possible. No one, I suppose, would deny that so far the practical men have had things pretty much their own way in this country—and what they have done with it Lewis has shown in Main Street and Babbitt.

There is no need of rehearsing in detail the panoramas of Gopher Prairie and of Zenith. Every one is familiar with their ugliness, dullness, hypocrisy, complacency, intolerance, standardization, conformity, inner emptiness, and discontent. Such is the society inevitably produced by whole-hearted devotion to making good, with a corresponding hostility to all activities which by their disinterestedness might interfere with that aim—a society in which science, art, and religion are prostituted and made bondslaves to practical success, in which poetry becomes heartening doggerel, orchestras are valued as municipal advertisements, and prayer is found to conduce to prosperity. Furthermore, it is a society which stunts and thwarts and starves all who are not in accord with its ethos, which produces Raymie Wutherspoons, Guy Pollocks, Chump Frinks, and Paul Rieslings. Of this society Arrowsmith also, though less exclusively satirical, is a satire, a national gallery of frauds and fakes; it contains, one might say, all Main Street and all Babbitt, and much more besides. It too will be valuable to

the future historian of the United States for its close observation and minute detail. Being a vertical rather than a horizontal view, it cuts across all strata of American life except that of the manual laborer, and is therefore more inclusive and more varied than the earlier books. Moreover, having a more sharply defined point of view, it is more positive, and it goes deeper, concerning itself less with the surface and more with a fundamental trait of the national character. It gains enormously from centering its focus, not on the exponents of social aberrations, but on an antagonist and to some extent a victim of them.

The chief importance of Arrowsmith, then, is that it shows the extreme difficulty of pursuing the creative or theoretic life in the United States. Furthermore, I should like to suggest that it establishes its thesis in two ways—not only by telling the story of its hero, but also by illustrating that of its author. As a writer Lewis has some curious traits, of which the most striking is his tendency to mimic or to imitate, to give a representation of reality which is the literary equivalent of glass flowers, Mme. Tussaud's waxworks, and barnyard symphonies. Closely allied are his dependence on his own experience and the care with which he gets up subjects, as he has got up medicine and bacteriology for Arrowsmith. All these characteristics, indeed, are abundantly manifested in his latest book; yet Arrowsmith is also the best proof that Lewis is capable of creative writing. It is much more of a novel than Main Street or Babbitt; in characterization, for instance, it is greatly superior. Leora, Martin's first wife, is by general consent Lewis's masterpiece in the creation of character. Not only is she likable, but she is indubitably real; though she is portrayed casually and without effort, no other character I know of in modern American fiction equals her in absolute final reality. And Martin suffers only in comparison with Leora; although far more difficult than either Carol or Babbitt, he is more understandingly and more successfully portrayed. Yet Martin is primarily a type, and reminds one of the preference which Lewis has shown in all his novels for types rather than individuals. It is characteristic of Lewis to care more for the representative of a class than for a single human being as a human being; even Leora interests him less than his typical fakirs in Arrowsmith. That may be why in general he contents himself with an external treatment of his characters, rarely manifesting much insight or sympathy or strength of feeling.

All these traits seem to point to a poverty of invention or of imagination—which in turn may be traceable to the influence of Lewis's environment. The growth of a creative mind is a dark and obscure subject, but the guess may be hazarded that the food on which the creative mind is nourished is experience and that a practical society operates in various ways to deprive it of that food. For one thing, the sensuous and aesthetic, the intellectual, above all the social experience which presumably is most vital to a novelist's development is simply not there—not in Gopher Prairie, for instance—to be had. But of even graver consequence is the effect of such surroundings on the artist's outlook or attitude. He needs to be receptive, to welcome experience, to be willing and able to surrender and abandon himself to it, forgetful of himself and absorbed by it. The fatal thing for him is to repel it, to be on his guard against it. But to wholly practical people any impractical person is ridiculous, possibly dangerous; and by their hostility they evoke in him an answering hostility; they make him assume a defensive attitude toward his environment. Yet for him to do so, for him to resist experience, is suicidal; unless he can let go and freely yield himself to it, his mind is denied its proper nutriment and cannot grow and mature to its full strength. This want of inner substance in turn may entail further consequences; it may lead to self-distrust, to undue self-consciousness, to a lack of integrity which appears as an unsettled, unstable point of view, to the assumption of alien standards in lieu of authentic personal standards. Besides developing a generally defensive attitude, an artist in a practical society, a society like that portrayed in Main Street, Babbitt, and Arrowsmith, is almost certain to return scorn for scorn, to seek an escape in the refuge of easy romanticism, or to try to deny his own nature and conform to the prevailing opinions.

Every point in the preceding could be profusely illustrated from the writings of Sinclair Lewis. For example, there is that uncanny knack of observation which enables him to mimic or to imitate so exactly to the life; this observation is as watchful as that of a wild animal on the lookout for its foes or as that of a Red Indian in the enemy's country. There is also his keen eye for inconsistencies or weaknesses in his prey—how quickly he pounces. Years of malicious scrutiny must have gone to the making of his last three volumes. Such observation is but one sign of a defensive attitude, an attitude which is also betrayed in the precautions he takes lest his readers misjudge him. He makes greater use of irony as a defensive weapon than any other writer I know of; he early made the discovery that if only he were ironical and showed that he knew better, he could be as romantic and sentimental and playful as he pleased. He writes as if always conscious of a hostile audience. He takes needless pains to make clear that he is more sophisticated than his characters, as if there were danger of our identifying him with them. He makes fun of their ingenuous enthusiasms, even when these enthusiasms have the best of causes. The result of it all is that often he seems unduly afraid of giving himself away.

In this respect he resembles his characters; nothing in them is more striking than their morbid self-consciousness. Only Will Kennicott and

Leora are free from it. The others are always wondering what people will think, always suspecting that they are the objects of observation and comment—and in Lewis's novels they are generally right. They are constantly posing and pretending, for the benefit even of waiters and elevator-boys. They do not dare to be natural; they are self-distrustful, uncertain, and insecure. They are self-analytical, and self-contemptuous for their lack of sincerity; yet they continue to pose to themselves, adopting one attitude after another. They have no inner standards of their own, because they are not integral personalities—they have not, in fact, developed any real personality at all.

Lewis himself shifts his point of view so often that finally we come to wonder whether he has any. One of the great advantages of Arrowsmith over its forerunners is that in it there begins to emerge an almost established point of view. Otherwise, one would be inclined to call Lewis a man of multiple personality—save that all these personalities have a look of being assumed for effect. All the Lewises are disdainful of each other. When he has been romantic, he throws in a jibe at sentiment lest we think him sentimental; when he has been cynical, he grows tender lest he be thought hard; when he has been severe with a member of the Babbittry, he emphasizes the virtues of the common people and the absurdities of highbrows and social leaders. All his manifold attitudes, however, may be reduced to basic ones: he is a romanticist, and he is a philistine—each bitterly satirical of the other. That is to say, he has tried to escape from his environment, and he has tried, with more success, to conform to it.

His romanticism is of two kinds. In the first place, there is in him much of the conventional romanticist and even of the sentimentalist. He has said of himself that he is "known publicly as a scolding corn-belt realist, but actually (as betrayed by the samite-yclad, Tennyson-and-water verse which he wrote when he was in college) a yearner over what in private he probably calls 'quaint ivied cottages.' " This is the Lewis who sympathizes with Carol in her dislike of Gopher Prairie and in her longing for "a reed hut built on fantastic piles above the mud of a jungle river," and who invents for Babbitt a dream of a fairy child playmate, "more romantic than scarlet pagodas by a silver sea." There is no essential difference between this romanticist and the more conspicuous one who has taken a tip from Arnold Bennett and gone in for the romance of the commonplace, although the latter despises the former. To establishing the strangeness and beauty of humdrum life Lewis devoted his first four books; he undertook to prove in Our Mr. Wrenn that a clerk's life in a Harlem flat is more romantic than travel in foreign lands, and in The Job that a stenographer is more romantic than Clytemnestra. This process is really no less an escape from reality than is the old-fashioned romance, for it consists, not in bringing out the essential quality and verity of ordinary life, but in casting a glamor over it and falsifying and sentimentalizing and prettifying it. The last three novels look as if most of the romance had worn off the commonplace, but there are traces of it, even in Arrowsmith.

Closely akin to the romanticist of the second sort is the Lewis who speaks as a man of the soil, one of the common herd, a Babbitt; he points out the essential goodness of small towns and their inhabitants and of boosters; he is homey and folksy, and strongly opposed to people whom he suspects of thinking that they are "superior." This side of Lewis is especially pronounced in the novels which preceded Main Street; long passages in them are sheer glorifications of Main-Streetism and of Babbittry. His whole tendency, when in this mood, is to strengthen and entrench the folk of Zenith and Gopher Prairie in their self-satisfaction and intolerance. In short, he is a philistine. He has not escaped contamination, he has partially conformed to his environment. He speaks, for example, its language. His technique of raillery he has learned from Sam Clark and Vergil Gunch; he merely turns their type of wit and humor back upon themselves; all his satire is a long tu quoque. His irony and sarcasm are of the showy variety popular on Main Street and in the Zenith Athletic Club. His style is founded on the uses of salesmanship, publicity, and advertising. He avails himself of all the tricks of a crack reporter to give a fillip to jaded attention. His people do not run, they "gallop"; instead of speaking, they "warble" or "gurgle" or "carol"; commonplace folk are "vanilla-flavored"; interior decorators are "daffodilic young men," "achingly well-dressed": dancing becomes "the refined titillations of communal embracing." No wonder Lewis has sold satire to the nation—he has made it attractive with a coat of brilliant if inexpensive varnish. The excellence of his rare intervals of real writing is lost in the general glare.

For there are such intervals; and they bring us back to Lewis, the artist, by no means insensible to beauty or devoid of the tragic sense of life. Save for bits of description and scattered passages, this Lewis was largely obscured in Main Street and Babbitt; yet no doubt he helped lend animus to the satire of that society which is so fatal to artists. Certainly to him the credit is due for Arrowsmith, the story of a man who would rather find out about things than make good. Yet even Arrowsmith, though an artist's as well as a scientist's book, is the work of a mangled artist. Perhaps after all it is better so: Lewis's romanticism and philistinism and vulgarity of style make him powerful because they make him popular. The attack on American practicality needs its shock troops—could we afford to give up so effective a critic for a better writer? Perhaps it is worth spoiling an artist to have him take so salutary a revenge. Lewis is the most successful critic of American society because he is himself the best proof that his charges are just.

# On *Arrowsmith*

## *by Mark Schorer*

Late in 1921, when Sinclair Lewis had nearly finished writing *Babbitt,* he wrote his publisher in New York that he thought that he would make his next novel "not satiric at all; rebellious as ever, perhaps, but the central character *heroic.*" His impulse to write a "heroic" novel may have arisen from a not uncommon criticism of *Main Street*—criticism that would be intensified by *Babbitt*—that Sinclair Lewis was without "spiritual gifts." And it might seem to point toward *Arrowsmith* (1925), which would indeed prove to be his next novel. In fact, Lewis was thinking about a labor novel, with a Christlike labor leader as his hero, and late in the summer of 1922 he went to the Middle West to talk to Eugene Debs, who was to be his hero's prototype, and to do other research in the labor field. In Chicago, through a medical friend, Dr. Morris Fishbein, he met a young bacteriologist named Paul de Kruif, and the two persuaded him that he was not really ready to write a novel about labor—as, indeed, he would prove never to be—and that instead he should write a novel about medical science. De Kruif would help him.

Medicine was an important profession in Sinclair Lewis's background. As a student at Yale, he had thought of it as a possibility for himself. His much respected older brother, Claude, was a surgeon in St. Cloud, Minnesota. His aging father, E. J. Lewis, was still practicing as a country doctor in Sauk Centre. A grandfather had been a doctor, and an uncle in Chicago was a doctor. Among Lewis's own earliest recollections, he said, were powerful impressions of medical practice.

A small boy whose memory is of being awakened by his father's talking to a patient, down at the door; of catching sleepy 3 A.M. phrases: "Where is the pain? Eh? Well, all right, but you ought to have called me earlier. Peritonitis may have set in." A small boy who was permitted to peep at

anatomical charts and ponderous medical books in The Office. Then his
brother going off to medical school—gossip of classes, of a summer's
internship, of surgery versus general practice. . . .

With such a background, the work and ideals of the doctors have
always been more familiar to me than any others, and when I began to
write novels . . . I thought of some day having a doctor hero. Part of
that ambition was satisfied in Dr. Kennicott, of *Main Street,* but he was
not the chief character, and furthermore I desired to portray a more
significant medico than Kennicott—one who could get beneath routine
practice into the scientific foundation of medicine—one who should
immensely affect all life.

Dr. Will Kennicott is a composite portrait derived from both the
author's father and his brother—perhaps more from the former than
the latter, although the latter was much like the former except that
he was more modern as a practitioner than either his father or Will
Kennicott. That kind of medical practice Sinclair Lewis, out of his
own experience, was perfectly equipped to handle in fiction, and it
appears again in some of the early portions of *Arrowsmith.* But about
experimental medical science, with which that novel was to be chiefly
concerned, he was completely ignorant, and, unless he undertook an
enormous amount of independent research, he could not have pro-
ceeded without the help of someone who was a master of this material.
For that reason, he drew up an agreement with Paul de Kruif, who
became, in effect, his research assistant, or, more exactly, his informant.

Paul de Kruif was perfectly equipped to help Lewis. He had been
a teacher of bacteriology at the University of Michigan, where he had
been associated with Dr. F. G. Novy (some of whose features were to
help make the composite character of Max Gottlieb) and had concentrated his research on immunology. He had served in the army as
a captain in the Sanitary Corps of the Medical Department, worked
on the poison and antitoxin of the bacillus of gas gangrene and made
the first prophylactic injections of gas gangrene serum. In the division
of pathology at the Rockefeller Institute, he had been research associate of the great Jacques Loeb (who provided the major features
of Max Gottlieb), and not only of Loeb, but also of Alexis Carrel,
J. H. Northrop (Terry Wickett, in part), and of others, all working
under the direction of Dr. Simon Flexner (A. DeWitt Tubbs). When
he met Lewis in Chicago, his connection with the Rockefeller Foundation had just been severed, as Terry Wickett's and Martin Arrowsmith's would be, after a row. Even these bare facts of the De Kruif
biography should indicate how much of his story became central to
Lewis's novel, and how indispensable he was to it.

Together, the two men set off on a freighter cruise of the West Indies. A plague on a tropical island—which would, of course, form the

climax of the novel—was the only certain situation that they had in mind to support the general theme that they had settled upon—of a young medical man who was average in his share of human limitations but remarkable in his dedication, in spite of all impediments and beguilements, to pure research. The purpose of the cruise was to assimilate the atmosphere of life in the islands of the Caribbean, but more than that, it was to educate Lewis in bacteriology and epidemiology and in the methods and spirit of research (for this they were equipped with a small library of medical textbooks and any number of letters of introduction to "tropical soldiers, doctors, and former pirates and brigands turned respectable"), and to work out on paper as complete an outline of the story as possible. When, after two months, they arrived in England, Lewis, with De Kruif still in attendance to assist whenever he needed technical aid, would sit down to the actual writing of the novel.

De Kruif served in a more imaginative capacity than that of mere technical informant. On the cruise, for example, one of his duties was to work out the complete professional histories of both Arrowsmith and Gottlieb, and to sketch those of lesser characters. From his own various experiences in medical science, he could produce prototypes that would suit the conflicts of the developing plot. With Lewis he would observe the men around them in search of proper physical types; thus they found Arrowsmith himself, "a grave black-haired youngster looking at us across his rum-swizzle glass in the ship's smokingroom."

Yet, for all the importance of Paul de Kruif's contributions to the material of *Arrowsmith,* it is interesting to note how much of Sinclair Lewis's background—and of his habit of satire—goes into it and how far advanced the novel is before the material in which De Kruif was particularly experienced comes into play. The novel opens with a fourteen-year-old boy in a small-town doctor's office: that is young Lewis himself in a somewhat more disorderly office than his father's. It proceeds to the medical school of the University of Winnemac, and the technical experience there could be largely his brother's, while the rather unpersuasive social experience—the fraternity life, the engagement to Madeline Fox, the Digamma Ball—are inventions in an area of experience that Lewis himself did not enter when he was at college. From Winnemac, Martin goes to Wheatsylvania, Dakota, to take up a country medical practice. Again, this material could derive entirely from his father's experience, and the general social environment is identical with that which Lewis had already so fully explored in *Main Street,* five years before. From Wheatsylvania, Martin proceeds to the medium-sized city of Nautilus, Iowa; and Lewis, with perfect tidiness, proceeds with him into the world of his next novel, *Babbitt,* the world of small-time hucksterdom. In Nautilus, Martin becomes involved, rather peripherally, in problems of public health, and with this material Paul de Kruif was no doubt of use, although it is hardly detailed enough to have demanded expert assistance. It carries Martin on, however, into an area of medical experience beyond simple practice, where external pressures are even more threatening to scientific purpose than they are to the physician.

It is only in Martin's next move, well after the middle of the novel, to the Rouncefield Clinic in Chicago, where he is employed as a pathologist, that the real story begins and that De Kruif became indispensable. The real story involves the conflict between an ideal of scientific research and the crass threats of commercial compromise with that ideal. The ideal had formed early in Martin's medical training at Winnemac and was consolidated when he became the assistant there to the great research scientist, Max Gottlieb. He had been deflected from his purpose into general medical practice through an unfortunate temperamental explosion of Gottlieb's and his own rash if happy marriage to Leora Tozer. (Leora, Lewis's most engaging heroine, was thought by his publishers to represent Lewis's idea of De Kruif's idea of his new wife; De Kruif had been married only a few days before they began their cruise, and his wife was with him in England while the novel was being written.)

While at the Rouncefield Clinic, operated by fashionable surgeons working for fashionable fees, Martin publishes a paper in a scientific journal that is seen by Gottlieb, now the great prima donna in the McGurk Institute of Biology in New York, and Gottlieb, after their long period of disaffection, summons Martin to him. With this reunion, Martin's ambition to become a pure scientist is consolidated and he undergoes what is nearly a ritual initiation into that pure world. The initiation occurs in a long speech by Gottlieb which ends as follows:

> But once again always remember that not all the men who work at science are scientists. So few! * * * To be a scientist is like being a Goethe: it is born in you. Sometimes I t'ink you have a liddle of it born in you. If you haf, there is only one t'ing—no, there is two t'ings you must do: work twice as hard as you can, and keep people from using you. I will try to protect you from Success. It is all I can do. So . . . I should wish, Martin, that you will be very happy here. . . .

It concludes five minutes later, when, alone, Martin ". . . prayed then the prayer of the scientist":

> God give me unclouded eyes and freedom from haste. God give me a quiet and relentless anger against all pretense and all pretentious work and all work left slack and unfinished. God give me a restlessness whereby I may neither sleep nor accept praise till my observed results

equal my calculated results or in pious glee I discover and assault my error. God give me strength not to trust to God!

The language is Sinclair Lewis's, but the terms of the dedication, like all the technical information with which the remainder of the novel is packed, he learned from or saw through the eyes of Paul de Kruif.

The remainder of the novel has to do, of course, with the internal politics of the McGurk Institute and the struggle of Gottlieb and Martin to preserve their ideals; the journey to the plague-stricken island and the death of Leora; Martin's triumphant return and his marriage to the wealthy and fashionable Joyce Lanyon; his rupture with the Institute and his separation from his wife and new child; his flight out of New York and out of society with one rough and ready but true friend who holds Martin's own ideals: the two of them in the Vermont wilderness where, unmolested, they will pursue their lonely truths.

It is a little fantastic, that ending, and quite unpersuasive. It comes out of Sinclair Lewis's own sentimental notions about the heroic life of untrammeled nature, of nature's noblemen. In spite of the fact that in *Babbitt* he had satirized the notion (for George Babbitt, too, was always yearning to get into the wild woods with one true friend), he presents it quite seriously here, and not for two fishermen but for two experimental scientists. (As if to prove the reality of his notion, Lewis himself, immediately after he had finished *Arrowsmith*, took a positively disastrous trip into the Saskatchewan wilderness; and then, in spite of the disaster wrote his melodramatic and idealized account of it in the novel, *Mantrap* [1926].)

One wonders if Paul de Kruif approved of the ending. If he did, a scientist, he was yielding to what must have been his training as a novelist while Lewis was being trained as a scientist. For even novels about science and about absolutely proved scientific fact must have an ending; but in this ending we have moved from science into what we can only call "science fiction."

Except for the ending, *Arrowsmith* is probably Sinclair Lewis's most firmly plotted novel. His fiction is not notable for its plotting. Both *Main Street* and *Babbitt* are loosely chronicled works with only the most wavering line of plot; their importance adheres in the observed details that the novelist can shore up against that line but that do not always have very much to do with it. In *Arrowsmith*, Lewis made a conscientious effort to give some dramatic coherence to his chronologically extensive materials. It is to be observed that the great majority of the important characters are involved in the relatively early Winnemac experience, and then that one by one these characters reappear in the later action, not always very persuasively, but at least reminding us, after Martin has moved so far, that way back there was Winnemac. And one might observe, too, the final section of the novel, which attempts a kind of reprise, or, more than that, a quick casting back over all the various scenes of which the plot has been played. If this device is in some ways mechanical, it nevertheless effects a loose knot-tying of what would otherwise be many flying strings.

One does not mean to suggest that the plotting of *Arrowsmith* is the chief reason for its success in either the commercial or the critical sense. *Arrowsmith* brought almost entirely new subject matter into American fiction. There had been earlier novels about doctors, and even, in Robert Herrick's novels, *The Healer* and *The Web of Life*, novels about doctors who vacillated between lucrative practice and professional integrity. Martin Arrowsmith, however, once he is on his way, is not primarily a doctor but a research scientist fighting for his different kind of integrity. Except for a minor character in Lewis's own story, "Number Seven to Sagapoose," written in late 1920, it is almost impossible to find such a figure in previous fiction. Martin Arrowsmith was a new hero, scientific idealism a new subject, and scientific individualism a new (and rather unscientific) perspective. And a Lewis novel was once again in the vanguard.

This new subject matter exists, however, within the familiar Lewis pattern: the young person who has his glimpse of values beyond the reach of the environment (in this case, beyond the reach even of the professional environment), his struggle to achieve it, his success after sacrifice. But the variations in the pattern made this novel seem almost to present a new Lewis: Arrowsmith *was* a hero, as earlier central figures had not been; the hero, after his human fumbling, acts on a platform of clearly defined affirmation; the hero can both love and give up love; the woman whom the hero loves is a heroine, one whom contemporary readers could themselves love and admire. Leora seemed to Lewis's readers to be a "realized" character, as no woman in his previous fiction had been, and she commanded their nearly universal praise.

Scientific research as a prominent strand in American culture has called up an ambiguous response. On the one hand, as Max Lerner has pointed out, it is the little understood object of fear, the interest of "queer geniuses" beyond comprehension, and in popular literature this response had long found itself in the notion of the "mad genius," sinister and beyond humanity yet tinkering with human destinies. (And Joyce, Martin's second wife, finally decides that he is "insane.") On the other hand, it had also increasingly become an object of in-ordinate respect, for men of science were truly "miracle men," and their work was profoundly involved with the national destiny. Thus, according to Mr. Lerner, "The American makes a cult of science as

a tribal symbol, just as he makes a cult of success as a personal symbol."
Lewis was the first novelist to exploit science as a tribal symbol; the
delightful irony, of course, is that he should have done so on behalf
of the personal symbol. Attacking materialism, he doubled his bank
account.

For *Arrowsmith* was another instant success, and this time without
the benefit of much controversy. If, here and there, some doctors
muttered in their beards (Joseph Collins, for example) that the novel
was only a "caricature" of certain features of the medical profession,
their murmurs of dissent were lost in the shouts of praise. *Arrowsmith*
stilled those carping voices that had complained that in *Main Street*
and *Babbitt* Lewis had failed to comprehend the American experience,
that he lacked "spiritual gifts," that he suffered from "inaccessibility
to a spiritual idea." Not only was *Arrowsmith* based on a "spiritual
idea"—selfless dedication to truth-seeking—it also permitted its chief
character to realize his "spiritual" ambitions, to transcend the strain
and the sordid struggle that, in *Main Street* and *Babbitt,* had defeated
the chief characters. Sinclair Lewis had recognized at last the best as
well as the worst in the American experience, and he was the most
American of American novelists.

Since *Arrowsmith* is still the most widely read of his novels, there
may well have been more than a little substance in this enthusiastic
acclaim.

# Martin Arrowsmith: The Scientist as Hero

## by Charles E. Rosenberg

With the manuscript of *Babbitt* almost complete in the fall of 1921, Sinclair Lewis already planned his next novel. "Perhaps," he wrote Alfred Harcourt, his friend and publisher, it would not be satiric at all, "rebellious as ever, . . . but the central character *heroic*." His next novel was *Arrowsmith*. Its heroic protagonist is a research scientist, the first of consequence in American fiction. To Sinclair Lewis he was far more than that.

Martin Arrowsmith is a new kind of hero, one appropriate to twentieth-century America. Journalists and historians tirelessly inform us that the 1920s were years of intense and aggressive materialism. Yet Arrowsmith is quite obviously a hero not of deeds, but of the spirit. His scientific calling is not a concession to material values, but a means of overcoming them. In the austere world of pure science and in the example of Max Gottlieb, Arrowsmith finds a system of values which guide and sanction his stumbling quest for personal integrity. It is this quest which provides the novel's moral structure. Martin Arrowsmith's professional career is the record of his deepening understanding and acceptance of these scientific values and of their role in assuring Arrowsmith's ultimate triumph in his struggles with a succession of increasingly plausible material temptations.

Other centuries have accepted patterns into which such moral achievement could be projected—the martyr, the pilgrim, the evangelist and, in more recent generations, the creative artist. None of these seemed particularly relevant to Sinclair Lewis in 1922. He had emphatically rejected the forms of traditional religion, despite the appeal which they had held for him as a lonely adolescent. Religion had become just another marketable commodity; its purveyors could not easily be pictured as heroic. Nor was the sensitive artist a potential hero; Lewis knew too many and knew them too well. Yet Sinclair

"*Martin Arrowsmith: The Scientist as Hero*" by Charles E. Rosenberg. From American Quarterly, *XV* (*1963*), *447-58. Copyright* © *1963 by the Trustees of the University of Pennsylvania. Reprinted by permission of the author and the University of Pennsylvania. Only one of Rosenberg's 30 extensive notes could be reprinted here.*

Lewis was very much a novelist of society, very much bound to the particular. His hero had to have a vocation. The problem was to find one in which dignity and integrity could be maintained in a world of small compromise and petty accommodation.

Yet America did have a heritage of dignity and individualism, Lewis believed. It lay in the pioneering spirit of the men and women who had settled the nation's West. Their heroic qualities had created America, yet theirs were the very characteristics which seemed to be disappearing most rapidly in a twentieth-century America, settled and implacably confining. *Arrowsmith* begins with an almost crudely pointed vignette: Martin Arrowsmith's great-grandmother, aged fourteen, is seated at the reins of a wagon. Her father, lying racked with fever in the wagon's bed, begs her to turn aside and ask shelter at her uncle's. But she will be obligated to no one and turns the wagon west. "They's a whole lot of new things I aim to be seeing," she exclaims. On the opening page of *Main Street,* Lewis describes another restless young girl. Carol Milford, like Arrowsmith, is the descendant of pioneers. Though the days of their exploits are "deader than Camelot," the spirit of her daring ancestors survives to animate this rebellious girl. In the future Mrs. Kennicott, however, the divine discontent which helped people a continent becomes an unfocused and almost pathetic dissatisfaction with the commonplace world of Gopher Prairie. Arrowsmith is gifted with the same vigor and curiosity—but is able to attain through it the heroic stature denied Carol. In the life of the pure scientist he discovers a vocation in which his spiritual endowments find meaningful and constructive expression.

During the early part of 1922, the *Century Magazine* published a series of anonymous articles attacking the pretensions of American medicine. The articles were entitled "Our Medicine Men," and written by Paul de Kruif, a junior staff member at the Rockefeller Institute. By the end of 1922 he was unemployed.

In the summer of 1922, Sinclair Lewis still sought a suitable protagonist for his heroic novel. He had begun his customarily detailed research for a novel of the American labor movement, its hero to be a Christlike leader modeled after Eugene Debs. But the novel did not seem to coalesce. On a hot August day in Chicago, Morris Fishbein, associate editor of the *Journal of the American Medical Association,* introduced Lewis to the young bacteriologist from the Rockefeller Institute. *Arrowsmith* was the result of this meeting. No one but Sinclair Lewis could have written quite such a novel, yet insofar as *Arrowsmith* is a comment on the world of American medicine and biological research, insofar as it makes use of scientific values and preoccupations, it reflects clearly the attitudes of Paul de Kruif.

De Kruif provided Lewis with the *vitae* for his principal characters, with the details of laboratory procedure and with a plausible scientific setting for Arrowsmith's exploits. Even more important, Lewis believed, was his contribution of the scientist's "philosophy." De Kruif entertained few doubts concerning the nature of the scientific endeavor or of the intellectual and personal integrity it demanded. He was equally certain that most American research was slipshod and careless, simply cluttering the journals and indices. De Kruif's influence can be documented not only in Sinclair Lewis' own words, but in the youthful bacteriologist's published writings. Before the appearance of *Arrowsmith* in March of 1925, he had written, in addition to the articles in the *Century,* an essay on Jacques Loeb which appeared in *Harper's* and the section on medicine, also anonymous, in Harold Stearns' *Civilization in the United States.* His discussion of Loeb, both in *Harper's* and in Stearns' *Civilization,* is particularly significant, for it is Jacques Loeb's values which are those professed by Max Gottlieb. De Kruif's "philosophy" is not a philosophy at all, but the recent convert's overenthusiastic reflection of a philosophy— of Loeb's biological mechanism.

Loeb's methodological scruples, even his style of life, had, moreover, a particular significance for American medicine in the early 1920s. He lived and expressed the gospel of pure science. In at least a limited sense, *Arrowsmith* is an incident in the birth of a new scientific medicine. De Kruif's hostility toward the medical profession is an extreme, though not unrepresentative, instance of the laboratory scientist's hostility toward the clinician. Such attitudes, formed in the uneasy co-existence between laboratory and clinical medicine, shaped many of the particular incidents and emphases in *Arrowsmith.*

Martin Arrowsmith's professional biography is a record not only of the progress of a confused and easily misled young man toward emotional and intellectual fulfillment; it is the recapitulation in one man's life of the development of medicine in the United States. Each stage of Arrowsmith's career corresponds to a particular stage in the evolution of American medicine. Doc Vickerson's practice—and Martin's own practice in Wheatsylvania—dramatizes, for example, the trials and rewards of what De Kruif called "the splendid old type of general practitioner." Both he and Lewis were sympathetic to this aspect of American medicine. It seemed informal, individual, at moments even heroic; at least it was free of that mixture of ersatz science and sordid commercialism which De Kruif regarded as having corrupted contemporary medical practice.

At Winnemac University, both teachers and classmates of young Arrowsmith exemplify particular types and trends in medicine's coming-of-age. Dean Silva, for example, the pious disciple of Osler and Laennec, represents the understanding and craftsmanship to be found in clinical medicine. Professor Robertshaw, the self-exiled Brahmin physiologist, who always spoke—with elaborate casualness—of his student days in Leipzig with Carl Ludwig, illustrates the transference of German laboratory medicine to the United States—and with his "fussy little . . . maiden-aunt experiments" proves that the progress of science demands the spirit and not simply the techniques of German science. Roscoe Geake, the professor of otolaryngology and future minion of the New Idea Instrument and Furniture Company, is a representative of the most sordid and ignoble aspects of clinical medicine, his specialism simply a device for the multiplication of fees.

Unlike most of his fellow medical students, Arrowsmith is the graduate of a four-year liberal arts curriculum. He is confident in his abilities as he enters medical school and looks forward to increasing his scientific knowledge. But, except for the inspiring example of Max Gottlieb, he is to be sadly disappointed. Arrowsmith's disillusionment is identical with that experienced by a hypothetical college graduate whose medical career was depicted by Paul de Kruif in the *Century*. He

> enters his first medical course with confidence, aware of his superiority over the majority of his fellows. It is easy, then, to imagine his dismay when he discovers that he knows far more of physics and chemistry than many of his medical instructors, and finds himself surrounded by glib-memoried, poorly-prepared ignoramuses who shine by reason of their parrot-like ability to reel off an enormous number of facts crammed out of text-books.

After a short residency at a metropolitan hospital, an experience which at first stimulates then bores him, Arrowsmith begins practice in Wheatsylvania, North Dakota. But a newly inspired enthusiasm for public-health work earns him only the scorn of the small farming community. Fortunately, he is able to leave. Through the agency of Max Gottlieb and Gustaf Sondelius, he obtains a position with the health department of a small Iowa city. In Nautilus, Arrowsmith's zeal quickly fades before the boosterism of his chief, the improbable Almus Pickerbaugh. Public-health programs, Martin discovers, are to be prosecuted in newspaper columns and on the lecture platform, not in the laboratory. De Kruif had, before meeting Lewis, recorded his intense dislike for such "shouters for public health," for these "dubious Messiahs who combine the zealous fanaticism of the missionary with the Jesuitical cynicism of the politician." Boards of health, he argued, should be administered by engineers, statisticians and bacteriologists —not by half-educated physicians.

Driven finally from his post in Nautilus, Arrowsmith is forced to accept a position with that "most competent, most clean and brisk and visionless medical factory, the Rouncefield Clinic." In the early years of the 1920s, the clinic seemed to all observers the most advanced form of medical practice. And De Kruif, like many other laboratory men, had already demonstrated his distaste for these gilded repair shops. Research, Arrowsmith soon learns, is regarded simply as a means of securing free advertising for the clinic. After a year of bondage at the Rouncefield Clinic, Arrowsmith's first paper is published in the *Journal of Infectious Diseases* and he is offered a research position at the McGurk Institute (of course, Lewis' conception of the Rockefeller Institute). At first Arrowsmith feels that he has reached a kind of scientific Elysium. He has a well-equipped laboratory, competent assistants, the company of his revered Max Gottlieb. Yet this too proves less than idyllic. Its demand for social graces, for premature publication, in short, its cultivation of success leads Arrowsmith toward his final and most important decision. He resigns from the Institute and joins his friend, the irreverent chemist Terry Wickett, who had already fled the compromising security of McGurk, at a wooded Vermont lake. Here, with a few like-minded investigators, they plan to conduct years of uninterrupted research. Thus the novel ends; Arrowsmith has conquered the final and most plausible obstacle in his quest for personal integrity—he has renounced success itself. Or at least success by the ordinary standards of American life. Like Max Gottlieb Martin Arrowsmith is destined for fame, but in a world whose judgments are eternal, international, and ultimately untouched by material considerations.

One of the tentative titles for *Arrowsmith* was *The Shadow of Max Gottlieb*. An unfortunate title perhaps, but in a way justified. For Gottlieb *is* the scientific vocation. He had, inevitably, to be German. It was not simply that Paul de Kruif was immensely impressed by Jacques Loeb. To the young men of Lewis' and De Kruif's generation, science was German science, its embodiment the German professor. Gottlieb is a symbol not only of the transfer of European knowledge and techniques to the New World, but an expression of the peculiar mystique of German academic life. His worship of research *qua* research and his reverent attitude toward this pursuit of knowledge are very much the product of the German university. Such beliefs never established themselves with quite such intensity in France, in England—or in the United States. Yet the almost religious texture of this attitude toward the scientist's task is essential to the moral structure of the novel. It clothes Arrowsmith's long hours in his laboratory with a spiritual, an inherently transcendent quality.

As in the legends of the saints, every sordid aspect of Max Gottlieb's life is only evidence of his grace and a comment upon the tawdry standards of those who mock him. He lives in a "small brown weedy" house, rides to his laboratory on an ancient and squeaky bicycle, and wears the shabby topcoat of a poor professor. Most Americans could only regard him as something of a crank. His was "no work for the tall man at a time when heroes were building bridges, experimenting with Horseless Carriages, writing the first of the poetic Compelling Ads, and selling miles of calico and cigars." Yet on the crowded desk in Gottlieb's little bungalow, letters from the "great ones" of Europe awaited his reply—and mocked the collective wisdom of Mohalis and Wheatsylvania and Sauk Centre. But Arrowsmith is vouchsafed the grace to understand and find inspiration in Max Gottlieb's life and ideas. Arrowsmith too shares something of his curiosity, something of his indignation at the shoddy and imprecise.

Sinclair Lewis created Max Gottlieb, but with raw materials provided by Paul de Kruif. Gottlieb, De Kruif later recalled, was an amalgam of Frederick G. Novy and Jacques Loeb. Novy was the austere and scientifically elegant professor of bacteriology at the University of Michigan who introduced De Kruif to biological research. Loeb was his idol at the Rockefeller Institute. Though Gottlieb is a bacteriologist and immunologist like Novy, not a general physiologist like Loeb, his personality and mannerisms obviously represent the novelist's rendering of the articulate and sardonic German—or at least the picture of him which De Kruif had presented to Lewis. In his recently published memoir, Paul de Kruif describes Gottlieb as a "muddy mélange" of Novy and Gottlieb. There is little evidence, however, of his having been dissatisfied with this sentimentally didactic figure when, in 1924, he first read the manuscript of *Arrowsmith*.

The genuine scientists in *Arrowsmith*, Gottlieb, Terry Wickett and Arrowsmith himself, all share the same conception of truth. It is knowledge obtained in rigidly controlled experiments, knowledge analyzed and expressed in quantitative terms. There is only one assurance in life, Gottlieb warns the youthful Arrowsmith: "in this vale of tears there is nothing certain but the quantitative method." Though many biologists today would approve such methodological sentiments, they would hardly express them with such passionate conviction. Our contemporaries are almost a century removed from the philosophical preoccupations which meant so much in Jacques Loeb's youth. The emotional intensity with which he, and his fictional counterpart Max Gottlieb, express such quantitative goals is clearly the reflection of an ancient conflict within the scientific community. This is the struggle between vitalism and mechanism.

Physical chemistry and mathematics were more than a method to

Jacques Loeb; they were his reason for becoming a biologist. He had, he recalled, read Schopenhauer and Eduard von Hartmann as a very young man. And while a student of philosophy at Berlin, the problem of free will seemed to him the most central of intellectual concerns. Loeb soon found himself unable to accept the existence of such individual freedom. Nor could he accept the techniques of philosophical analysis traditionally employed in the discussion of such problems. Loeb turned to physiological research in an attempt to prove that animal behavior was simply the sum of inorganic phenomena no different in kind from those studied by the physical scientist. Human behavior too, he believed, was no more nor less than the product of such physical and chemical forces. The "mystical" aspects of life were to be dissolved in the acid of mathematics and physical chemistry.

*Naturphilosophie* had been thoroughly vanquished by the late 1840s; yet the struggle against it had left a lasting impression on German biological thought. The men most articulate in opposing formal idealism were imbued with an instinctive sensitivity to philosophical implications and many embraced mechanistic materialism with an absolutist zeal inevitably paralleling the idealistic convictions of an earlier generation. It was this period of conflicting ideologies which shaped Loeb's intense and consistently generalizing mind.

Jacques Loeb was, for example, an assistant of Adolf Fick. Fick was one of the greatest of Carl Ludwig's students and perhaps the one most inclined toward the study of physiological processes in physical and mathematical terms. And Ludwig—with his great colleagues Helmholtz, du Bois-Reymond and Brücke—had been a leader in the struggle against a romantic or purely descriptive biology. Loeb himself always regarded the significance of his classic experiments on artificial parthenogenesis "to be the fact that they transfer the problem of fertilization from the realm of morphology into the realm of physical chemistry." His earlier investigations of animal tropisms were, he explained, crucial because they proved that animal movements were regulated "by the law of mass action." (Max Gottlieb remarks to Arrowsmith when the young man arrives at McGurk, that he hopes "to bring immunity reactions under the mass action law.") When Gottlieb feels that Arrowsmith has learned the elementary principles of his trade, he warns that true scientific competence requires a knowledge of higher mathematics and physical chemistry. "All living things are physico-chemical," he points out to his disciple; "how can you expect to make progress if you do not know physical chemistry, and how can you know physical chemistry without much mathematics?" Arrowsmith's maturity as a scientist comes only in the last few pages of the book. His papers are praised in Paris and

Brussels and Cambridge. But the socially impeccable Dr. Holabird is simply bewildered. "What," he asks, did Arrowsmith "think he was anyway—a bacteriologist or a biophysicist?"

In a very real sense, the values which sanction and direct Arrowsmith's quest for truth reflect those of Jacques Loeb and of a generations-old debate within the academic confines of German biology. As I have suggested, moreover, Max Gottlieb's values record accurately the laboratory scientist's impatience with the impressionistic and empirical aspects of clinical medicine. The physician could not, in the nature of things, be truly a scientist. The essence of medicine is the functional relationship which the individual physician bears to his patient. It is his task to heal—or at least to console. It is the scientist's task to understand. At best, De Kruif argued in 1922, the physician is a skilled technician of applied science. The attempt to train each practitioner as a scientist was simply delusive; a return to the preceptorial system of medical education would be preferable. Lewis too found it natural to accept the pure scientist's vocation as a higher one. The very social necessity which created the medical profession tied it to the exigencies of everyday life, to compromise and commercialism, to the collection of bills and the lancing of boils. As able, self-sacrificing and understanding as the best physician might be, he could never transcend the social relationships which formed the fabric of his professional existence. And to Lewis the essence of heroism, the gauge of a man's stature, lay in the extent to which he was able to disengage himself from the confining pressures of American society. His heroic protagonist had to be a scientist; he could not be a physician. And certainly not an American physician.

Both De Kruif and Lewis agreed that American society had debased even the pursuit of science. For both men the essential factor in scientific progress was the initiative and creativity of the individual investigator. There seemed increasingly little provision for such individualism in twentieth-century America. To De Kruif, no development within American science was more dangerous than its growing "barrack spirit." Centralization and bureaucratization of scientific research were not simply the inevitable concomitants of an increasing complexity within society and within the body of scientific knowledge —they were developments inimical to the impulse of spontaneous creativity. Hence Lewis' acid portraits of Rippleton Holabird, of A. De Witt Tubbs and of his League of Cultural Agencies. ("If men like Koch and Pasteur only had such a system," Tubbs bubbles to Martin, "how much more *scope* their work might have had! Efficient universal *cooperation*—that's the thing in science today—the time of this silly, jealous, fumbling individual research has gone by.") The young scientist, in an unfortuate image of De Kruif's, was to be denied the "privilege of wandering forth equipped only with the rifle of his intelligence, and thus to remain for long periods of lawless and impudent penetration of the forests and jungles of ignorance." No great man had ever drawn his inspiration from the memo pad of a research co-ordinator. Their hypotheses, De Kruif argued, were drawn directly from the observation of natural phenomena. The investigator who sought his inspiration in a library could hardly be considered a scientist at all.

Jacques Loeb was fond of aphorisms. He was especially fond of one coined by his friend and teacher, the great botanist Julius von Sachs. "All originality," Sachs observed, "comes from reading." Loeb was acutely conscious of history and of the communal nature of the scientific endeavor. He might mock the institutions of science and the mediocrities who so often found shelter within such institutional bulwarks, but he realized the futility of rejecting the scientific community as such. He died full of honors on the staff of the Rockefeller Institute. J. H. Northrop, model for Terry Wickett, even though a lover of the outdoors, always maintained his academic connections. Neither Loeb nor Northrop was a failure; neither renounced the corruptions of academic science and both learned to live with success. Even the criticisms and preoccupations of the restless Paul de Kruif were, as I hope to have shown, themselves characteristic products of the intellectual and institutional history of the biological and medical sciences. The conclusion of *Arrowsmith* is not only an indictment of the handicaps placed in the scientist's path by American society, it is a rejection at the same time of the scientific community whose values justify this indictment.

The novels of Sinclair Lewis are peopled with the wistful figures of Americans whose spiritual potentialities are unfulfilled. Arrowsmith is a conspicuous exception. Paul Riesling in *Babbitt* and Frank Shallard in *Elmer Gantry,* for example, were gifted with something of the sensitivity granted Arrowsmith. But unlike him, neither was able to enter a vocation in which his spiritual endowments could find expression. Their inability to conform brought only their own destruction. The tragedy of George Babbitt lies in the pathetic and overwhelming defeat administered his vague idealisms by the forces of organized Zenith. In the scientist's life, however, such chronic questionings find a recognized social function. Even Arrowsmith's social inadequacies, his lack of humor, his callousness toward the old and the lonely and the workingman are simply evidences of his spiritual stature. It is the small people who make good administrators, who are attuned enough to the petty circumstances of life to function successfully within them.

It is this pervading air of compromise which finally drives Arrowsmith from his wife, from his child and from his laboratory in New York.* His ultimate rejection of society and its demands has been criticized as callow romanticism—and perhaps it is. But it the logical result of Lewis' desire to depict greatness and his inability to conceive of its being allowed to exist within American society.

* The conclusion of Arrowsmith would, of course, seem particularly relevant to critics of a psychological persuasion. Arrowsmith's final decision is a rejection of maturity, of responsibility, of wife and child for an idyll with the virile Terry Wickett—an idyll sanctioned by the purity of Nature.

# *Arrowsmith* and *The Last Adam*

## by *William B. Ober, M.D.*

First, let us set down some facts. *Arrowsmith* (1925) was published after the success of *Main Street* (1920) and *Babbitt* (1922). Lewis was the most prominent American novelist of the day, writing at the peak of his powers, and had achieved international fame for his attack on the provincial fabric of the daily life of average citizens in the American Midwest. The novel was awaited with great expectation; after publication, it received high praise from almost every critic and reviewer. Ostensibly, Lewis was offered the Pulitzer Prize in 1926 for *Arrowsmith* but declined the award, and his refusal made headlines. *Arrowsmith* was a *Big Success*.

The central theme of *Arrowsmith* is Martin Arrowsmith's single-minded dedication to the ideals of medicine and medical research, an inspiring subject after the dull tawdriness of *Main Street* and *Babbitt*. Lewis rebutted his detractors who felt that he created his principal characters only to derogate them by depicting Martin Arrowsmith as one of nature's noblemen, a knight in shining armor. Speaking as a physician, I was delighted to see this book recently on the shelf of the Englewood, N.J. Public Library labeled Books for Young People. Medicine has it problems of recruitment as do other trades and professions. It is pleasant to think that after almost three decades *Arrowsmith* has the power to attract the adolescent mind and shape its aspirations and ideals.

Doctors had usually figured in fiction as secondary characters. *Arrowsmith* was the first novel I can think of in which the doctor's career is the main story line. Its success led to derivatives and imitations, ranging all the way down the scale from Sidney Kingsley's *Men in White* through a novel by A. J. Cronin, down to the films about Dr. Kildare, a number of radio serials, the comic strip about Rex Morgan, M.D., and reaching bottom in television's Ben Casey. Martin Arrowsmith has almost reached the status of an archetype.

"Arrowsmith *and* The Last Adam" *by* William B. Ober, M.D. *From* Carleton Miscellany, *IV* (*Fall, 1963*), *101-106. Copyright* © *1963 by* Carleton Miscellany. *Reprinted by permission of the publisher. Two paragraphs on* The Last Adam *have been omitted, as indicated by ellipsis.*

Re-reading *Arrowsmith* was a painfully embarrassing experience. Novelists who make a public show of realism (and *Arrowsmith* is a *roman à clef* based partly on the advice and acknowledged assistance of Paul de Kruif, a well-known bacteriologist formerly on the staff of the Rockefeller Institute) lay themselves open to the question (old as Dick's hat): Is it *True to Life?* Alas, on retrospect, it isn't.

The narrative technique is a chronological and anecdotal expansion of the character's experiences, but none of them exhibits appreciable intellectual or emotional growth. Lewis's vocabulary and sentence structure are well within the competence of any staff writer. Much of the dialogue belongs to "sentences we doubt ever were uttered"; his ear for speech is only fair. The style is intelligible but inexpressive. However, these weaknesses of Lewis's literary merits are well known. Where specifically, does *Arrowsmith* fall apart on analysis?

It is easy enough to point out that the minor characters are one-dimensional and drawn in the crude linear manner of a cartoonist. Max Gottlieb as the unworldly German scientist, Terry Wickett as the rebellious Young Turk of the research institute, Rippleton Holabird as the well-groomed scientific sharpshooter with no ideas of his own, Doc Almus Pickerbaugh as the orotund politician who eventually becomes a Congressman, all are paraded before us mouthing dialogue which could just as well be written in a balloon issuing from their mouths in a comic strip. Each secondary character has his assigned vice or virtue, a level of creative skill which is useful in scenario writing or in banging out religious allegories, but a good cut below a novel of realism.

The same bogus quality applies to Martin Arrowsmith. The only flaw in this scientist *sans peur et sans reproche* is that his gonads are occasionally stirred by the sight of a full bosom. However, he is never allowed to lapse from grace. In the novel we follow him from boyhood to the age of about forty; during this time his experiences of the world enlarge but he remains the same. The vitality of his first marriage to a plain girl from Wheatsylvania gradually declines as they have less and less in common. His second marriage to a wealthy, socially impeccable, and sexy wife terminates abruptly as he "chucks the whole show" for the Shangri-La of a two-man research lab in the Vermont mountains, scarcely a convincing denouement. Yet Arrow-smith's real failure is as a scientist. He is sent by his Institute to study the effects of bacteriophage on an epidemic of bubonic plague raging on an island in the West Indies. With the naive, well-intentioned *maladresse* of a rookie shortstop he fumbles the ball. This well-trained scientist from the McGurk Institute actually administers the treatment to the control group as well as the experimental group. What's more, nobody around has the brains to stop him. There is a limit beyond which each reader cannot voluntarily suspend his disbelief; my limit stems from almost 20 years in medicine and research; I cannot consider that episode a credible climax. Even granting that one could accept it, one would find that Martin Arrowsmith fails as a scientist even as he fails as a man, because he is in essence an unlettered, nonintellectual, undeveloping individual, and Sinclair Lewis has made him so. Far from being a credible or creditable hero, he behaves like a fool, yet we are supposed to clasp his image to our bosoms and morally profit from his example. George the Third may profit from his example, but I doubt that any embryonic doctors or researchers can. Martin Arrowsmith's scope may have sufficed for the 1920s, but it is ill-equipped for the more complex world of the 1960s.

None the less, it remains a popular book, and paper-bound editions sell well. For all its weaknesses and crudity, its lack of literary merit, it has a certain power, namely the attraction of the idea that men are willing to dedicate their lives to scientific research, a good deed in a naughty world.

It is true that many doctors are poorly educated except in their trade, and some may even be inept at that. I have met hundreds of doctors whose ignorance of the world outside medicine is incredible. It is currently fashionable to speak of the "tarnished image" of the medical profession. The shining armor is pitted and the gilt is off the gingerbread. Perfectly true, but up to a point. Some doctors are greedy and stupid; they drive big sleek automobiles and smoke big fat cigars; the AMA has all the warmth of U.S. Steel. On the other hand there are many doctors who are intelligent, well rounded, conversant with literature and the arts, who function constructively in their communities, and possess much of the maturity that Martin Arrowsmith lacks. Between the two extremes lies about 80 per cent of the profession, the gray, faceless multitude that constitutes the large majority of any segment of any society. I think one of the reasons the medical image is tarnished is that it was polished a bit too brightly. The radiance of the Holy Grail eludes almost all of us. Martin Arrowsmith's failure to fulfill the protocol of the plague-phage experiment can be partly attributed to his own lack of sophistication and his inability to set realistic, achievable goals for his experiment. The old maxim "Not failure but low aim is crime" is easily countered by "Don't bite off more than you can chew"—or "He who pisses into the wind will wet his breeches."

By way of contrast, James Gould Cozzens's *The Last Adam* (1933) received no fanfare when it appeared. It was one of Cozzens's earliest efforts. Unheralded by previous successes, it won no prizes. Although it is still in print, to my knowledge it has not appeared in a paper-bound edition. It is a *genre* piece dealing sympathetically with a number of the citizens of New Winton, a small town in Connecticut. The central figure is Dr. George Bull, a general practitioner of less than average skill and almost no industry, a physician whom I could not recommend to any patient who was even potentially seriously ill. He is depicted as a man who would rather hunt or fish, drink or fornicate than attend to the sick. Among his duties is the job of local health officer. He fails to inspect the latrine drainage from a temporary camp of workmen who are installing a large power line; the water supply of New Winton becomes contaminated, and an epidemic of typhoid fever breaks out. About 45 people are stricken and about 7 die. A town meeting is called to get rid of Dr. Bull on the grounds of ignorance, indifference, and incompetence. The move to oust him fails, partly because of collateral issues, but chiefly because the villagers recognize that human beings are imperfect creatures and are willing to accept the good with the bad, or some such truism. . . .

Honest craftsmanship and the reasonably close realization of an artistic goal are rather uncommon virtues when one views the bulk of literary and artistic output of a year or a decade, and it is much to Cozzens's credit that he was able to achieve this much at the beginning of his career. They are essential ingredients of any novel that aspires to greatness, the flour and butter of the pie crust. However, we look for additional qualities before bestowing accolades, and in this respect *The Last Adam* is insufficient.

Unlike *Arrowsmith* it is not likely to find its way on to the shelf of Books for Young People. It presents a segment of truth, somewhat unvarnished, but objective truth is not what librarians look for in "books that inspire." Nor do I think that the AMA will rate *The Last Adam* very highly; there are too many scabs on Dr. Bull's image. As a society we prefer our men in white to be as pure as St. George. We do not wish the dragon of disease to be fought off by a man with narrow shoulders on a lame horse with a flaccid lance. When Aristotle held the mirror up to nature, he did not specify that it be free from refractive error nor that the amalgam on its back be free from blemishes. In fact, in Aristotle's day mirrors didn't reflect properly, judged by present day optical standards. Maybe that's why he permitted himself this metaphor.

# Arrowsmith

## by D. J. Dooley

As in the preceding novels, Lewis has two intentions in *Arrowsmith*: to tell a story and to expose a situation. Here the two aims are closely linked, and the result is a much better plot than either *Main Street* or *Babbitt* possesses. The analysis of American medicine is just as interesting as the anatomy of the village or the city, and the conflict in which Martin Arrowsmith is engaged is far more gripping than the marital difficulties of Carol Kennicott or the rebellion of George F. Babbitt. The story gains enormously by having a central character who is clearly sympathetic to the author, instead of only doubtfully so; the reader can assume the normalcy of his point of view and laugh, weep, or deplore with him when he encounters examples of irrational or vicious behavior.

What way of life does Martin Arrowsmith seek to follow? There is no chance of his becoming an aesthete; Lewis makes him a man of action, suspicious of whatever may be effete and decadent, and clinches matters by giving the spokesman for literature the contemptible name of Brumfit and describing him as a literary playboy. When Martin examines religion as a guiding principle, Lewis's treatment is cavalier. Martin found himself viewing the cadaver he worked on "as a machine, fascinating, complex, beautiful, but a machine. It damaged his already feeble belief in man's divinity and immortality." The model of Christian behavior whom Martin meets at the University of Winnemac is a grotesque figure, the Reverend Ira Hinkley:

> He never ceased trying to stop their profanity. After three years on a backwoods football team he still believed that he could sterilize young men by administering reproofs, with the nickering of a lady Sunday School teacher and the delicacy of a charging elephant [18].

Having rejected the principles of this moral pest, Martin puts his faith in the scientism of Max Gottlieb, his instructor in bacteriology. There is nothing certain in life, says Gottlieb, except the quantitative method; employing it, he seeks to discover general laws governing natural phenomena in order to extend man's knowledge and develop new concepts of life. Following him, Arrowsmith embarks on "the search for the fundamental laws which the scientist . . . exalts above temporary healing as the religious exalts the nature and terrible glory of God above pleasant daily virtues" (120). Here is a good example of Lewis's prime rule for the handling of ideas: be brisk with them and count on the flow of words to sweep the reader right past their implications. Who could be so callous as to submit such a high-minded statement to analysis, to ask whether contemplatives really consider that the glory of God makes the practice of the virtues of little account, to question the validity of a scientist's belief that the cure of the sick is of small consequence in comparison with the search for the fundamental laws of nature? Lewis gives the impression of having gone deeply into the problem of the rational foundation for devotion to science, but there is more appearance than reality. He gives Martin's position no metaphysical basis, in fact, no sanction outside itself; furthermore, it seems to be undermined by a radical skepticism, not a mere withholding of judgment:

> She had called Martin a "lie-hunter," a "truth-seeker." They decided now, talking it over in their tight little two-and-a-quarter room flat, that most people who call themselves "truth-seekers"—persons who scurry about chattering of Truth as though it were a tangible separable thing, like houses or salt or bread—did not so much desire to find Truth as to cure their mental itch. In novels, these truth-seekers quested the "secret of life" in laboratories which did not seem to be provided with Bunsen flames or reagents; or they went, at great expense and much discomfort from hot trains and undesirable snakes, to Himalayan monasteries, to learn from unaseptic sages that the Mind can do all sorts of edifying things if one will but spend thirty or forty years in eating rice and gazing on one's navel.
>
> To these high matters Martin responded, "Rot!" He insisted that there is no Truth but only many truths; that Truth is not a colored bird to be chased among the rocks and captured by its tail, but a skeptical attitude toward life. He insisted that no one could expect more than, by stubbornness or luck, to have the kind of work he enjoyed and an ability to become better acquainted with the facts of work than the average job-holder [271].

Does this leave Martin with any better reason for acting than the "mental itch" he derides? If truth is nothing more than a skeptical attitude towards life, why not be skeptical about the value of scientific research?

It is interesting to observe that Lewis gains support for Martin's position partly by caricaturing alternatives to it, partly by associating with it moral and intellectual attitudes which the reader is likely to favor (honesty, open-mindedness, a disposition to question received opinions, and so on), and partly by attaching religious overtones to it. He gives it prestige, if not an intellectual defense. The comparison of the scientist to the religious occurs many times. Science is the new religion to supplant outmoded creeds, and Gottlieb is its prophet; Arrowsmith says, "You think Gottlieb isn't religious, Hinkley. Why, his just being in a lab is a prayer" (30). Like the Messiah, Gottlieb has to endure scorn and ignominy:

> Not once did he fail to be hated by his colleagues, who were respectful to his face, uncomfortable in feeling his ironic power, but privily joyous to call him Mephisto, Diabolist, Killjoy, Pessimist, Destructive Critic, Flippant Cynic, Scientific Bounder Lacking in Dignity and Seriousness, Intellectual Snob, Pacifist, Anarchist, Atheist, Jew [124].

Gottlieb himself refers to great scientists as though they were members of a priesthood or a religious order: "Father Koch and Father Pasteur and Brother Jacques Loeb and Brother Arrhenius." In a moment of spiritual rapture, Martin composes a scientist's prayer which concludes with the paradox "God give me strength not to trust to God!" In the manner of Comte, Lewis tries to ennoble science by referring to it in religious terms and to present it as a worthy successor to religion as an object of mankind's devotion.

The novel might be described as an anatomy of the obstacles in the scientist's way. They are put there by the medical profession, by the character of the scientist himself, by various social groups, and by the general outlook of the American people. Almost all the possible attitudes toward research are presented, and each one is supported or illustrated by an impressive amount of detail. The Main Street view is shown when Martin goes to Wheatsylvania, North Dakota; here the doctor is a medicine man and conformity to the tribal code is much more important than medical skill. The view of Babbitt's friends is shown when Martin gets a job in Nautilus, Iowa, another Zenith: "The only difference between Nautilus and Zenith is that in both cases all the streets look alike but in Nautilus they do not look alike for so many miles." Here the Public Health Director must be a Booster and not a conscientious pursuer of germs; in fact, the worst mistake he can make is to try to clean up dirty houses or dirty restaurants owned by influential citizens. Everywhere, it seems, the Boosters overcome the Truth-seekers. Pharmaceutical houses are so unscrupulous that they market preparations even before they have been tested and continue to sell them after they have been proved useless; clinics are mere medical factories which will tolerate no research nonsense; and even genuine research organizations are only the playthings of so-called philanthropists.

All these are valid subjects for satire. But the last great obstacle to scientific asceticism, humanity, is not. Should the quest for scientific knowledge override every other human consideration? In Gottlieb's life, it does. Martin decides in favor of humanitarianism when he abandons his controlled experiment on St. Hubert during an epidemic and administers his serum to everyone, but he regards himself as a traitor to science. At the end, he casts everything else aside for the sake of research. The pursuit of truth to the exclusion of error is clearly something desirable; the pursuit of scientific truth to the exclusion of all human values is something else again. We have moved, therefore, from an area in which satire attacks deviations from a reasonable, normal position to an area in which there is a dramatic tension between two kinds of value. But the transition is not awkward; the central character this time does not make an unpredictable change, and the book does not break in two like *Main Street* and *Babbitt*.

But it does have two types of characters—the realistic and the unrealistic. The latter can be identified by their comic-strip names. Martin works under Dr. Rippleton Holabird in a research institute headed by Dr. A. De Witt Tubbs and financed by Capitola McGurk, the Great White Uplifter. Earlier he has served under Dr. Almus Pickerbaugh, dynamic Director of Public Health in Zenith, Booster extraordinary, and father of the Healthette Octette—eight strapping girls floridly ranging from Orchid to Gladiola. Through this brilliant caricature, Lewis shows that the archetypal qualities of the Booster—brashness, vulgarity, hatred of nonconformity, worship of success—are as conspicuous in the world of medicine as they are in real estate and advertising. Yet Lewis's use of such comic-strip characters would seem to give the lie to those who consider the primary quality of his work its documentary veracity of photographic realism. For the moment, it is perhaps sufficient to observe that Lewis's use of characters with extravagant names and personalities is not necessarily an error in artistic judgment: these parodies or travesties of human beings illustrate his contention that America, in seeking to develop a new kind of person, has only turned out new specimens of the grotesque. . . .

In showing what had happened in one field of endeavor, Lewis was describing the failure of the epic dream: America had aspired to be a nation of free individuals, but the worship of material success by the many had forced the few independent spirits to turn their backs on their fellow men. Carl Van Doren said that readers found in the story a familiar American pattern of behavior. Despairing of medical practice because of its confusions and compromises, Arrowsmith forsook it to do his true work in a wilderness, "almost exactly as Leatherstocking and Daniel Boone had in the eighteenth century turned away from the corrupted settlements to be themselves beyond the tumult of mankind." Arrowsmith is aware of his resemblance to other types of pioneer; when he explains to Joyce, his wealthy wife, that he is going to escape from the captivity which her way of life imposes on him, he refers to "those of us that are pioneers." In fact, the pioneering theme is established in the opening scene of the novel, which depicts the intrepid determination of Arrowsmith's great-grandmother in the Ohio wilderness.

Arrowsmith's mental make-up is derived from the pioneer ethos at least as much as from Max Gottlieb. Maxwell Geismar is dubious about the scientific skepticism of the novel and would prefer to call it a fashionable cynicism, but actually Martin holds to the tradition of dissent which Geismar describes in his *American Moderns* as perhaps the most vital element in American democracy:

> Gradually Martin's contemplation moved beyond Almus Pickerbaugh to all leaders, of armies or empires, of universities or churches, and he saw that most of them were Pickerbaughs. He preached to himself, as Max Gottlieb had once preached to him, the loyalty of dissent, the faith of being very doubtful, the gospel of not bawling gospels, the wisdom of admitting the probable ignorance of one's self and of everybody else, and the energetic acceleration of a movement for going very slow [228].

We have seen that Lewis is so much of Geismar's mind regarding the tradition of dissent that near the end of *Main Street* he makes institutions rather than individuals responsible for everything he has satirized. The truest American, in his view, is the aloof, independent, egocentric, suspicious pioneer. So strong is his emphasis on isolation that—as Geismar stresses, though Raymond H. Palmer said it long before him —he nowhere gives a picture of a true home or a true church or a true corporate life of any kind; he has taken the tradition of dissent to its logical and ultimate conclusion. As Raymond Williams states in a discussion of Dickens, there is always a system of some kind, and the argument against system per se is usually either fretful or ignorant. This type of anti-institutionalism seems to be the retained position of the adolescent, the innocence which essentially rejects the adult world. On the evidence of Lewis's life and writings, Palmer is justified in calling him "the great undisciplined American, the apotheosis of American individuality and irresponsibility." *Arrowsmith* is thus a paradoxical combination of an attack on conditions which inhibit scientific progress and a flight from maturity, a plea for a return to a simpler and more uncomplicated way of life than the modern world can offer. . . .

*Arrowsmith* has been one of the most highly praised—some would say overpraised—of Lewis's works. To many reviewers it was either a genuine step forward by its author or conclusive proof of his excellence as a novelist. Its weaknesses, however, have become more apparent with the passing of the years. Many male readers seem to have fallen in love with Leora: Harcourt called her "just about the best woman character in American fiction that I know of." But Martin Light thinks her quite incredible—chiefly a convenience who does all the right things, especially in never interfering with her husband's plans, and who tops it all off by becoming a martyr to science. He is equally unimpressed by the character of Arrowsmith; although Lewis says that he matures, he doesn't show it, and his tone throughout remains that of an exuberant schoolboy. A similar criticism was made by Warren Beck in a notable attack on Lewis's reputation. He grudgingly allowed that Arrowsmith was one of the two consistent characters Lewis had created—Babbitt was the other—but maintained that Lewis had failed to control him: "He has run off not only with many a reader but with his author, for in glorifying Arrowsmith as scientist Lewis seems unaware of what a crude and lopsided human being he had made of him." Arrowsmith as doctor has been both criticized and defended; perhaps the most famous criticism is that by Hans Zinsser, in *Rats, Lice and History,* to the effect that if an epidemiologist on a plague study behaved in the manner of Arrowsmith he would be regarded by his associates as a yellow ass and a nuisance.

De Kruif, giving a verdict "aged in the wood of my head over many years," does not criticize Arrowsmith so much as Gottlieb, whom he considers a muddied mélange of his own scientific mentor and of Jacques Loeb, "who was my master in a philosophy of the mechanistic conception of life, of God a mathematician, of God a Univac, of God a superstition, of God a childish concept, of God nonexistent." This conception, he writes, accorded with Lewis's own philosophy. For Loeb, it was undoubtedly the product of considerable reflection about causality, creation, the existence of matter, and related topics. But when Lewis writes, "Like all ardent agnostics, Martin was a religious man," it is obvious that there is not very much deep reflection behind the remark; it is merely a glib paradox designed to give an appearance of profundity. Light finds the heroic pretensions of the novel embarrassing, in view of the slick-magazine language of many of its passages; when Lewis writes that Martin "was homesick for the laboratory, for the thrill of uncharted discoveries, the quest below the surface and beyond the moment," we feel, as we did about Babbitt's dreams of his fairy child, that the whole thing is overwritten and slickly contrived. In spite of the excellence of much of the satire and the author's success in fusing satire and novel, the book shows that Lewis could not do what [Stuart P.] Sherman asked him to do—give a satisfactory exposition of values.

# The Best of the Great Decade

## by Sheldon N. Grebstein

As for the significance of such a novel [as *Arrowsmith*] to Lewis's own experience, we need not look very far. Lewis has left us this account in his own words:

> A small boy whose memory is of being awakened by his father's talking to a patient, down at the door; of catching 3 A.M. phrases: "Where is the pain? Eh? Well, all right, but you ought to have called me earlier, Peritonitis may have set in." A small boy who was permitted to peep at anatomical charts and ponderous medical books in The Office. Then his brother going off to medical school—gossip of classes, of a summer's internship, of surgery vs. general practice. And behind father and brother, a grandfather and uncle who were also doctors.
>
> With such a background, the work and ideas of doctors have always been more familiar to me than any others, and when I began to write novels . . . I thought of some day having a doctor hero. Part of that ambition was satisfied in Dr. Kennicott of "Main Street," but he was not the chief character, and furthermore I desired to portray a more significant medico than Kennicott—one who could get beneath routine practice into the scientific foundation of medicine—one who should immensely affect all life.

Lewis's idealistic intentions and high purposes for his book are unmistakable here. *Main Street* and *Babbitt* had also been motivated by idealism, but the noise of their satire and the weight of their social criticism had obscured this. Lewis now wanted to do an affirmative book, one in which he could express his idealism openly. He wrote to Harcourt of his desire, even before he had decided definitely on the subject of the book: "I think I shall make my next novel after Babbitt not satiric at all; rebellious as ever, perhaps, but the central character *heroic*."

Indeed, Martin Arrowsmith was to become the symbol of an ideal,

"The Best of the Great Decade" by Sheldon N. Grebstein. From Chap. III, "The Great Decade," of Sinclair Lewis (New York: Twayne Publishers, Inc., 1962), pp. 86-96. Copyright © 1962 by Twayne Publishers, Inc. Reprinted by permission of the publisher. Grebstein's seven footnotes have been omitted.

the modern reincarnation of the American pioneer spirit, which was to Lewis among the most vital of our native traditions. The novel's opening paragraph, with its portrait of Arrowsmith's pioneer great-grandmother, contains the spirit of intrepidity later to prevail in Arrowsmith's quest for truth. The grandmother's courageous rejection of the immediate and practical, in order to seek the distant and un-known, foreshadows the book's theme: "Nobody ain't going to take us in," she says to her sick father, who wants her to turn the wagon toward relatives living nearby. "We're going on jus' as long as we can. Going West! They's a whole lot of new things I aim to be seeing!" Just as his forebears had in this spirit settled the physical frontier, Arrowsmith explores the frontiers of knowledge.

It is also obvious from the start that this novel will be another of Lewis's tales of self-realization. In each of the novel's basic situations Arrowsmith meets society and is defeated by it, but in each case he surmounts the defeat by growing, by learning from his mistakes. In each of these encounters and defeats he leaves society a little further behind, until, finally, he abandons it completely. The subtitle of the book could well be "All for Truth, or, the World Well-lost."

*Arrowsmith* could also be read as a highly moralistic allegory, some-what reminiscent of *Pilgrim's Progress*, with Martin a twentieth-century version of the man of piety in pursuit of the twentieth-century deity, scientific truth; or as a modern Red Cross Knight, the cross, in this case, that we associate with the saving of lives. He is the best sort of character Lewis can make him and still remain within the realm of realism; he is human, at times petty and selfish in his personal relationships, tactless, stubborn (two of Lewis's early titles for the novel, "The Stumbler" and "The Barbarian" suggest this phase of the hero), but he is noble in his ideals, ambitions, career.

In his portrayal of Arrowsmith, biographical parallels exist between Arrowsmith and his creator. In Arrowsmith's case, when marriage becomes a barrier to work, he gives up marriage, and the same situa-tion may have applied to Lewis. Certainly, in writing *Arrowsmith* he was separated from his wife and son for even longer periods than usual and at a time when the marriage was already in jeopardy—partly because of Lewis's already-exercised conviction that he needed complete freedom from familial obligations to write.

We cannot help speculating about yet another possible parallel, the one between Arrowsmith's career and Lewis's. Wherever Arrowsmith goes, he makes enemies and becomes notorious not only for the frank-ness with which he announces his opinions of what is good and what is bad but also for his well-intentioned but unpolitic attempts to do the right thing, to make people better. They think of Martin as a radical, a crank, while at heart he is sincerely altruistic. The same might be said of Lewis and his books. Ultimately, Arrowsmith stops trying to *like* people and be liked by them because, as in Lewis's case, he *loves* them. He cannot, as Lewis could not, accept, excuse, tolerate, gloss over. He wants to uproot, change, reform—and his motivation is love. Lewis, too, loved America without liking her, just as he loved the small town and Babbitt without approving of them.

Gottlieb, whom some critics have found the novel's most memorable character, is no less essential than Arrowsmith to its theme. In Gottlieb Lewis created for the first time an almost wholly admirable figure, a man the reader can revere as the embodiment of all the chief virtues Lewis respected: integrity, true intellectual attainment, a total inability to compromise by accepting unfinished or imperfect work. Gottlieb, a man at the farthest remove from the affable and well-adjusted good fellow, is the kind of man who carries civilization on his shoulders. He is a pessimist who voices his doubts about the possibility of progress and about man's superiority to animal, yet his own genius advances progress and proves man's superiority. He declares himself an agnostic, but his purposes, his work, and his very name belie this assertion. Joining with Arrowsmith and Gottlieb as truth-seekers, and sharing in their merit, is Terry Wickett, a minor although memorable character.

Set in contrast to this heroic triumvirate are Duer (again notice the characternym), who represents hard, professional competence operating solely on the profit motive; Pickerbaugh, the expert in promotion and self-promotion, a Babbitt of public health; and Holabird, the scientist turned administrator and empire-builder, the intellectual fraud. The novel's female characters also fit into its allegory and strengthen the pattern of contrast which we have come to recognize as basic to Lewis's books. Madeline Fox, Martin's first love, belongs to the type whose ancestress is Istra Nash* and whose last descendant is Olivia Lomond (*World So Wide*). Joyce Lanyon, rich, cultured, sophisticated, sexually alluring, is an extension of Madeline and a direct forebear of Fran Dodsworth. In their demands upon Arrowsmith, Madeline and Joyce symbolize the demands of Society and Success. In opposition to them Lewis places Leora, the Western girl, and the prototype of Lewis's good women: quiet, long-suffering, plain, utterly loyal, a little dumb, totally and selflessly dedicated to her husband's fulfillment. She represents personal integrity. The two different kinds of women in *Arrowsmith* summarize more emphatically than in any other of Lewis's books, with the exception of *Dodsworth,* the continuous conflict between what might be called the *hausfrau*

---

* A chic, exotic bohemian for whom the hero briefly carries a torch in *Our Mr. Wrenn;* she reappears in *The Trail of the Hawk* as a potential mismatch for Carl Erikson. [R.J.G.]

and the debutante; and *Arrowsmith* is one of the few novels in which the hero makes the right choice.

To view *Arrowsmith* as purely a morality play, and its characters as mere abstractions, is to view it in distorted perspective, however. Despite Lewis's original intention to make it an affirmative book, sharp satire and social criticism are in evidence. Lewis's heaviest barrage falls upon the commercialism, quackery, pseudo-science, and glory-hunting in medical education, medical practice, and medical research. Beginning with Martin's college and medical school career, which permits Lewis a number of shots at the American university and the professional school, Lewis then moves his hero first to a prairie town, next to a small midwestern city, and at last to Chicago; and all the while he peppers away at targets already riddled in *Main Street* and *Babbitt*.

In these experiences as small-town general practitioner, city public health director, and member of a famous clinic, Arrowsmith is confronted by the same problems facing Carol and Babbitt: if he is to be successful, prosperous, and accepted, he must lie, dodge, compromise, do the expected and profitable. His attempts to reform the health habits of both town and city are nearly as clumsy and ill-advised as Carol's efforts to bring culture to Gopher Prairie and as Babbitt's rebellion; and, like them, he is defeated. Lewis also uses Gottlieb's career as a source of satire and social commentary. Through him we see how genius is feared and thwarted in academic life and how talent is less important than affability, when Gottlieb is driven out of his university position by lesser men. We see the exploitation of the many for the profit of the few in Gottlieb's employment by a large pharmaceutical manufacturer who pressures him to discover a new serum so that the company may monopolize its sale, charging all that the traffic will bear.

Finally, in his depiction of the McGurk Institute Lewis's satire reaches into the top levels of the world of science. It is lamentable, although not unthinkable, that commercialism, venality, and fraud should exist in universities, medical schools, medical practice, public health, and private clinics; but an endowed institute, devoted to pure, non-profit research, ought to be paradise. However, here, too, Arrowsmith finds corruption. Not only are the staff members put on public display by the vain lady whose husband supports the institute, there are also internal politics, intrigues, cliques, jockeyings for position and, worst of all, pressure from the administration to publish for the sake of publication and fame, even though the experiments may not be finished. Only Gottlieb, Wickett, and Arrowsmith are devoted to their work for its own sake. The others coast on reputations earned long before, or they spend their time and energy parading as scientists rather than laboring as scientists. Most are also astonishingly ignorant of anything outside their own specialties. Above all, the McGurk Institute serves to demonstrate the perils of success.

With his discovery of the "X" principle, Martin for the first time experiences Success, which will bring him every possible benefit except the chance to do his work. He finds even a little taste of it heady wine, but he is saved from its influence when a foreign scientist anticipates his discovery in a published paper. The full and deadly power of Success and Position falls instead upon Gottlieb, who is given the directorship of the institute, is immediately caught up in its dissensions, and is ruined as a scientist. There is perhaps a parallel in this situation with Lewis; he, too, had known success and enjoyed its gifts. Perchance he had begun to fear it and its effects upon his work.

The satire and the social criticism in *Arrowsmith* are supported by a solid underlayer of fact. Almost all of Lewis's books, including the poor ones, have this foundation; it gives them a satisfying density and bulk, and nowhere is this truer than in *Arrowsmith*. In it the details of a medical training and internship, of a general practice, of the job of the public health official and the operation of a private clinic, the secrets of the research laboratory, and the hazards of the battle against epidemic are all tremendously appealing to the reader. Americans are worshipers of science but they also distrust certain aspects of it—as they distrust any work which tends to isolate the worker and which depends upon abstract thought. Thus, of all sciences we distrust medicine least because the doctor is a familiar figure. He produces visible, practical, desirable results, and it is possible for the layman to apprehend and admire the doctor's skill in much the same way he would admire the skill of an engineer. Furthermore, the doctor himself justifies the mysteries of research, for we tend to see the medical laboratory and medical research not as Science, distant and unknown, but as manufacture, the production of necessary goods. It is not difficult to understand, then, why medical books and medical novels have been enormously popular in America. *Arrowsmith* both perpetuated and shared the public's enthusiasm for such books. It brought to the reader that especially comforting thought that he was being educated as well as entertained, so that even the most puritanical or pragmatic could not feel that he was fiddling away his time with a storybook.

Beginning with *Main Street* Lewis had given his readers the titillating sense of being on the "inside," a sense which is heightened by *Arrowsmith* because the inside is now that of a hallowed profession, rather than the depressing detail of life as lived in the small town or by the average businessman. Consequently, while Lewis's appraisal of American civilization as manifested in Wheatsylvania, North Dakota, or Nautilus, Iowa, is hardly more complimentary than it was in *Main Street* and *Babbitt, Arrowsmith* did not arouse the public furor that the others did—except for a mild fuss among some members of the medical profession. Both the novel's pervading idealism and its sober factuality overweighed its satire and brought it success, without the success of scandal.

The book's narrative component is also superior to those of *Main Street* and *Babbitt,* for the story moves beyond the conflicts of the hero with his social environment and centers upon the doctor's war against death. More varied in locale and character, more crowded with dramatic incident, swifter in movement, *Arrowsmith* is always interesting. When, in the last quarter of the book, death enters as an antagonist in the Plague, the story becomes gripping. Almost as good is the previous section, which recounts Arrowsmith's discovery of the "X" principle. In this section Lewis captures the intensity and joy of pure research and the conjunction of circumstance and prescription, fate and free will, in the quest for some of the secrets of life itself. While Lewis never attains the profundity and multiplicity of suggestion of a Kafka, a Dostoevsky, a Faulkner (he does not belong in their rank), this grappling with the universal is a rare thing in his work; on this occasion, at least, he climbs above his usual range. In short, *Arrowsmith* demonstrates more of Lewis the philosopher than any other novel.

The crucial issue in the Plague episode is the giving of serum under test conditions—the problem of carrying out a controlled experiment when men's lives are involved—in order to answer the scientific question of the accuracy of Arrowsmith's research and of the serum's worth. But the scientific question includes the human question of whether to let thousands die now so that millions may be saved later. Experimental verification becomes, therefore, more than a matter of scientific curiosity. This is the conflict which Martin must resolve and which he is not strong enough to do. His humane feelings prevail, and by this lapse Martin overturns the course of his whole career, one in which he had in every previous crisis resisted the public's demands at his own expense but for the public's greater good. Ironically, this climactic failure brings Arrowsmith fame and adoration at the same time that his conscience is being eaten away by his knowledge he has failed as a scientist. The Plague stops, whether through the effectiveness of the serum or of its own accord Arrowsmith will never know; another doctor records the experimental data Martin should have set down; and Arrowsmith returns to America a hero. As a final irony, Martin's scientific conscience, Gottlieb, the one man who would have immediately perceived and announced his failure, has suffered a mental collapse and does not even recognize him. The McGurk Institute, as we by now expect it to do, squelches Martin's report that there is insufficient evidence of his serum's value and instead releases an optimistic statement.

The final clash between science and society occurs in Martin's marriage to the rich, beautiful, and suave Joyce Lanyon. Through her Arrowsmith is exposed to and temporarily persuaded by the temptations of wealth and luxury and the responsibilities of father-hood. Yet we know that sooner or later Arrowsmith, like the Lewis rebel he is and like Lewis himself, will find respectability intolerable. The arguments between Martin and Joyce resolve into a single argu-ment and a single choice: whether to be decent, responsible, and civilized, or to be free to work. Joyce's parting shaft at Martin, after he has rejected her final attempt at reconciliation and a final appeal to his sense of duty as a father, is completely accurate. She calls him a fanatic. He is indeed a fanatic; he has left behind all common sense. But in Lewis's terms and in the novel's terms, that is the better way. While the other men Arrowsmith has known—the righteous, the hypocritical, the conniving—enjoy success and prosperity, he is shut away in Vermont with Terry Wickett, where he plans pre-doomed researches into insoluble problems. However, in his experimenter's utopia in the Vermont woods, removed from humanity save for a few other dedicated *isolatos* and severed from all intercourse with a corrupt society save for the necessity to do just enough commercial work to support pure research, he has at last found independence and maturity as a scientist—so Lewis tells us.

The basic conflict in *Arrowsmith* has become a staple of much recent literature and sociological analysis (for example, *The Lonely Crowd*), and it expresses what is also apparently a basic problem in twentieth-century America: whether to be *liked*—that is, whether to be amiable, to be well rounded, to leave plenty of time for family, recreation, friends—or do one's work. To do one's work, as Lewis structures the situation, means to neglect family and friends, and to be hard, tough, honest, and crude. Furthermore, the man who does his work and is responsible only to its demands, is inevitably and necessarily hard to like. As Lewis portrays Gottlieb, Arrowsmith, and Terry, the only three true scientists in the novel, they are all men who make enemies far more readily than friends, men who can be understood and appre-ciated only by another of their own rare breed.

This is the definition of the true scientist which Lewis conveys in *Arrowsmith*. He is: (1) utterly dedicated to his discipline; (2) thor-oughly educated in all branches of science and not just in his own specialty; (3) an artist in his techniques and methods; that is, he does his work beautifully; (4) unwilling to publish his findings until he is absolutely sure they are completely validated; (5) harshly self-critical; (6) much more concerned with the demands of day-to-day work than with the philosophical or metaphysical meaning or ultimate application of his discoveries, but not unaware of their possible benefits to mankind; (7) fundamentally motivated by a great love for mankind, but it is well disguised, even totally hidden, under a cynical and tough exterior; (8) too concerned with his work to be concerned with the niceties of social behavior or even his duties as father and husband, yet human enough to want and need a wife, children, friends; (9) above all, cautious of success, position, prestige, because nothing can ruin a scientist more quickly, and no one, not even a Gottlieb, is proof against them.

To the problems of marriage and success, Lewis seems to present these solutions: first, the scientist must have a wife, children, and friends who are totally permissive and understanding, who will always be there when he needs them but not there when they might be in the way. Second, the best and perhaps the only possible way to forestall the dangers of the World is to get away from it, to seek isolation. The novel's final conclusion implies, therefore, that the scientist is truest to himself and to mankind when he rejects his own humanity. A provocative implication, it has taken on significance in the years since *Arrowsmith*, for it bears on such topical issues as interspace travel, nuclear explosions, germ warfare, and, in short, on the entire relationship of scientists, scientific principles, and scientific discoveries to the future of the human race. It is too large a question to debate here.

Lewis's definition of the scientist may be approached, however, from another and more limited point of view. In the excitement of the story and in Lewis's contrast of good and bad characters—Leora and Joyce, Arrowsmith and Holabird—we are at least temporarily convinced that easy living, gracious manners, recreation, and high position inevitably lead to mediocrity and failure in real accomplishment. Upon reflection, we wonder whether that is true; whether creative activity is possible only under Thoreau-like conditions, and whether there is so close an association between pure research and asceticism as Lewis declares. We also wonder whether it takes any more time to be pleasant than rude when the scientist does present himself in public. It may be conceded to Lewis that the scientist who is working for the public good must and should on occasion bully and command rather than wheedle and coax, but we wonder if Lewis pays too little credit to the public's intelligence. After all, thousands volunteered to cooperate in tests of the Salk vaccine.

Whatever their answers, the questions *Arrowsmith* raises are not trivial. Many of the points it makes are the same as those in *Main*

*Street* and *Babbitt,* but they are made in a more artistic manner. Heavier weight is carried by the novel's characterizations and action and less by Lewis's tirades, sermons, and monologues. Although the situation is somewhat the same—the individual struggling for self-fulfillment and integrity in a society which wants to keep things as they are and which demands of us above all that we be nice— *Arrowsmith,* unlike *Main Street* and *Babbitt,* has no compromise at the end. The hero wins his fight against himself and against the world; he becomes a scientist, solitary, dedicated, skilled. He makes a separate peace on his terms, not the world's. Actually he is able to do so because, however much it may deride him, the world needs him, and both he and the world know it. The same was not true of Carol and Babbitt. Once isolated from their society, there would be no place for them to go except, perhaps, to Europe.

As in all Lewis's work, *Arrowsmith* blends realism, satire, and romance. The realism is conveyed by the hard core of scientific knowledge in the novel and by the presence of death. The satire appears in the struggle between the society and the individual. The romance enters into the exaggerated, even fabulous portrayals of such characters as Sondelius and Leora (we like Leora far better than Joyce, but Joyce seems more credible); into the black and white conflict between Science and Success; and into the near-melodrama of some of the book's incidents. Withal, *Arrowsmith* is marred by fewer flaws than either *Babbitt* or *Main Street.* It does not have *Main Street's* tedious repetition and occasional hysteria; it avoids *Babbitt's* flatness. The satire is less heavy and obvious. The tone and movement of the novel are swifter, surer, more inspired than in either of his previous triumphs.

Moreover, we are heartened by Lewis's unqualified enthusiasm for science, the true hero of the book. In *Arrowsmith* there is no confusion about Lewis's standards or loyalties. Gottlieb and Arrowsmith are unequivocally gallant and admirable characters whose weaknesses are far less than their strengths. Here we *know* where Lewis stands, for the novel has the consistent frame of reference too often missing in his work. All in all, *Arrowsmith* shows Lewis's growth as an artist; it is the best novel of his great decade and it is among the better American novels written in this century.

# Why Sinclair Lewis Got the Nobel Prize

## by Erik Axel Karlfeldt

This year's Nobel prize winner in literature is a native of a part of America which for a long time has had Swedish contacts. He was born at Sauk Centre, a place of about two or three thousand inhabitants in the great wheat and barley land of Minnesota. He describes the place in his novel "Main Street," though there it is called Gopher Prairie.

It is the great prairie, an undulating land with lakes and oak groves, that has produced that little city and many others exactly like it. The pioneers have had need of places to sell their grain, stores for their supplies, banks for their mortgage loans, physicians for their bodies and clergymen for their souls. There is cooperation between the country and the city and at the same time conflict. Does the city exist for the sake of the country, or the country for the city?

The prairie makes its power felt. During the winters, long and cold as ours, terrific storms dump their snow in the wide streets, between low and shabby houses. The summer scorches with an intense heat and the city stinks,* because it lacks both sewers and street cleaning. But yet the city, of course, feels its superiority; it is the flower of the prairie. It has the economic threads in its hands and it is the focus of civilization; a concentrated, proud America amidst these uncouth serfs of foreign origin, Germans and Scandinavians.

Thus the city lives happily in its self-confidence and its belief in true democracy, which does not exclude a proper classification of the

*"Why Sinclair Lewis Got the Nobel Prize"* by Erik Axel Karlfeldt, trans. by Naboth Hedin. Originally published with Lewis's acceptance speech in pamphlet form (New York: Harcourt, Brace & World, Inc., 1930), pp. 1-8. Copyright 1930 by Harcourt, Brace & World, Inc. Reprinted by permission of Naboth Hedin.

* Here Dr. Karlfeldt is in error. Although the prairie villages of the Middlewest had, in my time, no sewers or street-cleaning, each house excellently took care of its own sewage, and despite the summer heat of which he speaks, the predominant smell was of wild roses, millions af acres of wheat, and that indefinable scent of a great farming land.—Sinclair Lewis.

people, its faith in a sound business morality, and the blessings of being motorized; for there are many Fords on Main Street.

To this city comes a young woman, filled with rebellious emotions. She wants to reform the city, inside and out, but fails completely and comes near perishing in the attempt.

As a description of life in a small town, "Main Street" is certainly one of the best ever written. To be sure the city is first and foremost American, but could, as a spiritual milieu, be situated just as well in Europe. No one of us has suffered as much as Mr. Lewis, however, from its ugliness and bigotry. The strong satire has aroused protests locally, but one does not need to be keen-sighted to see the tolerant strain in this sketch of his native town and its people.

Back of the puffed-up complacency of Gopher Prairie lurks, however, jealousy. At the edge of the plain stand cities like St. Paul and Minneapolis, already little metropolitan centers with their skyscraper windows gleaming in the sunlight or the evening's electricity. Gopher Prairie wants to be like them and finds the time ripe for a campaign of progress, based on the rising war price of wheat. A stump speaker is imported, a real rabble-rouser of the peppiest kind, and with blatant eloquence he demonstrates that nothing will be easier than for Gopher Prairie to take the lead and arrive in the 200,000 class.

Mr. Babbitt—George Follansbee Babbitt—is the happy denizen of such a city. It is called Zenith, but probably cannot be found on the map under this name. This city with its enlarged horizons here-after becomes the starting point for Mr. Lewis's critical raids into the territories of Americanism. The city is a hundred times as large as Gopher Prairie, and, therefore, a hundred times richer in hundred per cent Americanism and a hundred times as satisfied with itself, and the enchantment of its optimism and progressive spirit is embodied in George F. Babbitt.

As a matter of fact, it is probable that Babbitt approaches the ideal of an American popular hero of the middle class. The relativity of business morals as well as private rules of conduct is for him an accepted article of faith and without hesitation he considers God's purpose with man to be that he should work, increase his income and enjoy modern improvements. These commandments he feels he obeys and he therefore lives in complete harmony with himself and society.

His profession, real estate, is the highest in existence, and his house near the city, with its tree and lawn, is standard, inside and out. His motor car is of the make that corresponds to his position and in it he whizzes throught the streets, proud as a young hero amidst the dangers of traffic. His family life also corresponds to the bourgeois average. He has a wife who has become used to his masculine grumblings at home, and the children are impertinent, but that is what one expects. He enjoys excellent health, is well-fed and thriving, alert and good-natured. His daily lunches at the club are feasts of instructive business conversations and stimulating anecdotes; he is sociable and winning. Babbitt is furthermore a man with the gift of speech. He has learned all the national slogans and whirls them about with his flowing tongue in his popular talks before clubs and mass meetings. Not even for the most elevated spirituality does he lack sympathy. He basks in the company of the noted poet, Cholmondeley Frink, who concentrates his genius on the composition of striking, rhymed advertisements for various firms and thereby earns a good annual income.

Thus Babbitt lives the life of the irreproachable citizen conscious of his respectability. But the jealously of the gods broods over a mortal whose happiness grows too great. A soul such as Bibbitt's is, of course, incapable of growth; it is a ready-made article from the start. Then Babbitt discovers that he has tendencies toward vice which he has neglected—but not wholly, one ought to add. As he approaches fifty, he hastens to make up for the neglect. He enters an irregular relationship and joins a frivolous gang of youths, in which he plays the role of a generous sugar daddy. But his deeds find him out. His lunches at the club become more and more painful through the silence of his friends and their aloofness. They give him hints that he is spoiling his chance of future membership in the committee of progress. Here it is naturally New York and Chicago that loom before him. He then succeeds in recovering his better self and it is edifying to see him kneel in the sacristy of his church, where the pastor gives him absolution. And then Babbitt can once more devote himself to the Sunday school and other socially useful activities. His story ends as it began.

That it is institutions as representatives of false ideas that Mr. Lewis wants to get at with his satire, and not individuals, he has indicated. It is then a triumph for his art, a triumph almost unique in literature, that he has been able to make this Babbitt, who fatalistically lives within the borders of an earthbound but at the same time pompous utilitarianism, an almost lovable individual.

Babbitt is naive and a believer, who speaks up for his faith. At bottom there is nothing wrong with the man and he is so festively refreshing that he almost serves as a recommendation for American snap and vitality. There are bounders and Philistines in all countries and one can only wish that they were all half as amusing as Babbitt.

To the splendor of the figure, as well as that of other speaking characters in the book, Mr. Lewis has added his unparalleled gift of words. Listen, for example, to the conversation of a few commercial travelers, sitting together in a compartment of the express to New York. An unsuspected halo falls over the profession of selling. "Their romantic hero was no longer the knight, the wandering poet, the cowpuncher, the aviator, nor the brave young district attorney, but the great sales manager, who had an Analysis of Merchandising Problems on his glass-topped desk, whose title of nobility was 'Go-getter,' and who devoted himself and all his young samurai to the cosmic purpose of Selling—not of selling anything in particular, for or to anybody in particular, but pure Selling."

"Arrowsmith" is a work of a more serious nature. Lewis has there attempted to represent the medical profession and science in all its manifestations. As is well known, American research in the natural sciences, physics, chemistry and medicine, ranks with the best of our age, and it has several times been greeted as such from this very plat-form. Tremendous resources have been placed at its command. Richly endowed institutions work without ceasing on its development.

That even here a certain number of speculative persons want to take advantage of their opportunities may be regarded as inevitable. Private industries are on the alert for scientific discoveries, and want to profit by them before they have been tested and finally established. The bacteriologist, for instance, searches with infinite care for vaccines to cure widespread diseases and the chemical manufacturer wants to snatch them prematurely from his hand for mass production.

Under the guidance of a gifted and conscientious teacher, Martin Arrowsmith develops into one of the idealists of science, and the tragedy of his life as a research worker is that, after making an im-portant discovery, he delays its announcement for renewed tests until he is preceded by a Frenchman in the Pasteur Institute.

The book contains a rich gallery of different medical types. There we have the hum of the medical schools with their quarreling and intriguing professors. Then there is the unpretentious country physi-cian, remembered from "Main Street," who regards it as an honor to merge with his clientele and become their support and solace. Then we have the shrewd organizer of public health and general welfare, who works himself up into popular favor and political power. Next we have the large institutes with their apparently royally independent investigators, but under a management which to a certain extent must take into consideration the commercial interests of the donors and drive the staff to forced work for the honor of the institution.

Above these types rise Arrowsmith's teacher, the exiled German Jew, Gottlieb, who is drawn with a warmth and admiration that seem to indicate a living model. He is an incorruptibly honest servant of science, but at the same time a resentful anarchist and a stand-offish misanthrope, who doubts that the humanity whose benefactor he is amounts to as much as the animals he kills with his experiments. Further we meet Gustaf Sondelius, a glorious Titan, who with singing and courage pursues pests in their lairs throughout the world, exterminates poisonous rats and burns infected villages, drinks and preaches his gospel that hygiene will kill the medical art.

Simultaneously runs the personal history of Martin Arrowsmith. Lewis is much too clever to make his characters without blemish and this man Martin suffers from faults which at times seem obstructive to his development, both as a man and as a scientist. His best help as a restless and irresolute young man he gets from a little woman he has encountered at some hospital where she was a nurse, and he begins to drift about the country as an unsuccessful medical student; he looks her up in a little village in the far west, and there she becomes his wife. She is a devoted and simple soul who demands nothing and who patiently waits in her solitude when, bewitched by the siren of science, her husband loses himself in the labyrinths of his work.

Later she accompanies him and Sondelius to the pest-infected island where Arrowsmith wants to test his serum, and her death in the abandoned hut, while her husband listens distractedly to another and more earthy siren than that of science, seems like a poetically crowning final act to a life of primitive self-sacrificing femininity.

The book is full of admirable learning which is certified by experts as accurate. Though master of light-winged words, Lewis is least of all superficial when it comes to the foundations of his art. His study of details is always careful and thorough as that of such a scientist as Arrowsmith or Gottlieb and in this work he has built a monument to the profession of his own father, that of the physician, which certainly is not set up by a charlatan or a fakir.

His big novel "Elmer Gantry" is like a surgical operation on one of the most delicate parts of the social body. Presumably it would not pay to search anywhere in the world for the old Puritanical virtues, but possibly one might find in some of the oldest corners of America a remnant of the sect which regarded it as a sin to re-marry, once it had pleased God to make one a widower or widow, and wicked to lend money at interest. But otherwise America has no doubt had to moderate its religious rigidity. To what extent a preacher like Elmer Gantry is common over there, we cannot here have the slightest idea. Neither his slap-dash style of preaching with his cocky pugilistic manners—"Hello, Mr. Devil"—or his successful collecting of money and men inside the gates of the church, can hide the sad fact that he is an unusually foul fish and Mr. Lewis has neither wished nor been able to give him any attractive traits. But as description the book is a feat of strength, genuine and powerful, and its full-flavored, somber satire has a devastating effect. It ought to be unnecessary to point out that hypocrisy thrives a little everywhere and that any one who attacks it at such a close range places himself before a hydra with many heads.

Sinclair Lewis's latest work is called "Dodsworth." Of the family we have previously caught glimpses in his books as one of the most aristocratic in Zenith—a circle where no Babbitt ever gains admission. "Most aristocratic," probably often means in America "richest," but Sam Dodsworth is both aristocratic and rich. He notices even after 300 years the English blood in his veins and wants to know the land of his ancestors. He is an American, but not a jingo. With him travels his wife, Fran. She is already over forty, while he is fifty. She is a cool beauty, "virginal as the West wind," though she has grown children. In the European atmosphere she blossoms out as a brilliant flower of luxury, reveling in vanity, pleasure and selfishness. She goes so far that the quiet man who loves her must leave her to her fate.

But once alone he meditates on the problem "Europe-America," and as a real business man he wants to clear up his accounts with both. He thinks of many things, honestly and without prejudice. One of his observations is that the very soil in Europe has some of the old-time quiet, which America, the land of restless record-hunters, lacks. But America is the land of youth and daring experiments. And when he returns there, we understand that the heart of Sinclair Lewis follows him.

Yes, Sinclair Lewis is an American. He writes the new language—American—as one of the representatives of 120,000,000 souls. He asks us to consider that this nation is not yet finished or melted down; that it is still in the turbulent years of adolescence.

The new great American literature has started with national self-criticism. It is a sign of health. Sinclair Lewis has the blessed gift of wielding his land-clearing implement, not only with a firm hand, but with a smile on his lips and youth in his heart. He has the manners of a pioneer. He is a new builder.

# Sinclair Lewis and the Revolt
# from the Village

## by Carl Van Doren

American fiction had regularly celebrated the American village as
the natural home of the pleasant virtues. Certain writers, aware of
agrarian discontent or given to a preference for cities, might now and
then have laid disrespectful hands upon the farm; but even these
hesitated to touch the village. It seemed too cosy a microcosm to be
disturbed. There it lay in the mind's eye, neat, compact, organized,
traditional: the white church with its tapering spire, the sober school-
house, the smithy of the ringing anvil, the corner grocery, the cluster
of friendly houses; the venerable parson, the wise physician, the canny
squire, the grasping landlord softened or outwitted in the end; the
village belle, gossip, atheist, idiot; jovial fathers, gentle mothers, merry
children; cool parlors, shining kitchens, spacious barns, lavish gardens,
fragrant summer dawns, and comfortable winter evenings. These were
images not to be discarded lightly, even by writers who saw that time
was discarding many of them as industrialism went on planting ugly
factories along the prettiest brooks, bringing in droves of aliens who
used unfamiliar tongues and customs, and fouling the air with smoke
and gasoline. E. W. Howe in *The Story of a Country Town* had made
it plain enough that villages which prided themselves on their pioneer
energy might in fact be stagnant backwaters. Mark Twain in *The
Man That Corrupted Hadleyburg* had put it bitterly on record that
villages too complacent about their honesty might have become a
hospitable soil for meanness and falsehood, merely waiting for the
proper seed. Clarence Darrow in his elegiac *Farmington* (1904) had
insisted that one village at least had known as much restless longing
as simple bliss. But the revolt from the village which brought a new

*"Sinclair Lewis and the Revolt from the Village"* by Carl Van Doren. From
The American Novel, 1789-1939, *(New York: The Macmillan Company, 1921; rev.
ed., 1940), pp. 294-95 and 303-314. Copyright © 1940 by Carl Van Doren. Reprinted by permission of the Estate of Carl Van Doren. The first two paragraphs
are taken from Chap. XVI on the "Revolt," and the remainder from Chap. XVII
on Lewis; omissions are indicated by ellipses.*

tone into American fiction was most dramatically begun by Edgar Lee Masters's *Spoon River Anthology* (1915).

Though it was not a novel, it was the essence of many novels. Masters had imagined a graveyard such as every American village has and had furnished it with epitaphs of such veracity as no village ever saw put into words. The epitaphs seemed to send up a shout of revelation. Readers felt that they had sat down to an incomparable feast of scandal. The roofs and walls of Spoon River were gone and the passers-by could look into every room; the closets were open and all the skeletons rattled; brains and breasts had unlocked themselves and set their most private treasures out for the most public gaze. Masters was particularly outspoken about love, which had rarely been so secretive anywhere as in the American villages of fiction. But about all aspects of behavior in his village he was impatient, if not violent, toward cautious subterfuges. There is filth, he said in effect, behind whited sepulchres; drag it into the light. Spoon River is slack and shabby. Nor is its decay chronicled in any mood of tender pathos. It has been a general demoralization. Except for a few saints and poets, whom Masters hailed with lyric ardor, the people are sunk in greed and hypocrisy and apathy. While inwardly the village dwindles and rots, outwardly it clings to a pitiless decorum which veils its faults till it can overlook them. Again and again the poet went back to the heroic founders of Spoon River, to the days of Lincoln whose shadow lies little heeded across the sons and daughters of meaner days. The town has forgotten its true ancestors. . . .

*Spoon River Anthology* had been a collection of poems, *Winesburg, Ohio* a collection of short stories. *Main Street* (1920) was in the more customary and popular form of a novel, and it carried the protest against the village to an immediate, immense audience. A brief passage in the book became a classic for the decade. Village contentment, the passage ran, was "the contentment of the quiet dead, who are scornful of the living for their restless walking. It is negation canonized as the one positive virtue. It is the prohibition of happiness. It is slavery self-sought and self-defended. It is dullness made God." There was, another passage said, a village virus that "infects ambitious people who stay too long in the provinces." Hundreds of thousands were not content, the book insisted. They were only silent. The book broke up the conspiracy of silence, and the revolt from the village swept across the whole country, with acrimonious attacks and defenses.

It was often charged that Lewis had followed the lead of *Spoon River*. He had in 1920 not even read the book, and his own dissatisfaction with dry provincialism went back to his youth. He was born in 1885 in Minnesota, son of a country doctor who had come there from New England. In the small town of Sauk Centre (original of

Gopher Prairie) the romantic boy resented it that Minnesota had no Robin Hoods nor Ivanhoes nor Round Tables. At Yale he found it was not the mellow community he had expected. He held himself chafingly aloof, belonging to no societies, making few close friendships, prowling at night through the back quarters of the town. He first appeared in print with a poem on Lancelot, in the college magazine. In the summers of 1904 and 1906 he went to England on cattleboats. During the summer vacation of 1905 he worked in Sauk Centre on a novel to be called *The Village Virus* which he did not finish but which was the preliminary version of *Main Street.** Instead of returning to Yale for his fourth year he spent two months in a socialistic colony in New Jersey, founded by Upton Sinclair, and left it for New York, where Lewis lived in the slums writing sentimental verse. Neither socialism nor Bohemianism satisfied him. He traveled steerage to Panama, to be like one of the dashing heroes of Richard Harding Davis, but came back to Yale to finish the work for his degree in 1908. This year was pleasant, and for a time he thought of going on to become a doctor of philosophy and then a professor of English somewhere. Instinct drove him to more active courses. He became in turn editor of a small newspaper in Iowa, charity worker in New York, reporter in San Francisco, editor in Washington of a magazine for teachers of the deaf. From 1910 to 1915 he was in New York again at various kinds of work for various publishers. Then, supporting himself with stories for magazines, he lived for another five years in Florida, Chicago, Minnesota, New York, Cape Cod, with a motor trip half across the Continent. In Washington he settled down long enough to write *Main Street,* and from its reception discovered that at thirty-five he held up to American what it took, or angrily refused to take, as a mirror to its nature.

Lewis early changed from sentimental verse to realistic-satirical prose, but his novels were his poems in the sense that autobiographical experience lay behind each of them, though none of them was actually autobiographical. The hero of *Our Mr. Wrenn* (1914) is a lonely, restless minor clerk in New York who escapes from his routine life long enough to go to Liverpool on a cattleboat and have timid adventures in exciting England. Una Golden in *The Job* (1917) has to continue in a dreary office such as Lewis hated. He understood them because he had been close enough to their lives to sympathize with them, perhaps in fear that he himself might never rise from those monotonous levels. In *The Trail of the Hawk* (1915), one of the earliest novels with an aviator for hero, Hawk Ericson, born in Minnesota, sud-

---

* Lewis later said he had worked on the novel then; his diary for 1905 shows that he had only begun to think about it. [R.J.G.]

denly leaves college for Panama, learns to fly in California, marries
a bewildering girl in New York, finds a settled existence unendurable,
and runs with her away from dullness. *Free Air* (1919) goes over the
route by which Lewis had motored from Minneapolis to Seattle,
and in the Minnesota hero and the Brooklyn heroine represents the
difference in manners which had made the young Lewis self-conscious
in New Haven and New York.

In *Main Street* he set out to tell a true story about the American
village, whether anybody would read it or not, and he was surprised
by the tremendous acclamation. He had not reasoned that it was
time to take a new attitude toward the village or calculated that it
would be prudent. He only put down, dramatically, the discontents
that had been stirring in him for at least fifteen years. But there was
something seismographic in his nerves, and he had recorded a ground
swell of popular thinking and feeling. His occasional explicit comments on dull villages were quoted till they reverberated. Many
readers thought there were more such comments than there were.
The novelty was less in the arguments of the book than in the story.
That violated a pattern which had been long accepted in American
fiction. The heroes of Booth Tarkington, for instance, after a brief
rebellion of one kind or other, came to their senses and agreed with
their wiser elders. But Carol Kennicott, rebelling against the unnecessary ugliness of Gopher Prairie and its smug stodginess, and
in the end having to yield to it, yet appears as a heroine. Her discontent has been not folly but a virtue. The village is the villain.

The characters of the story, even Carol, are not remembered as
Gopher Prairie is. The most famous incident is Carol's first walk
along Main Street, with its detailed description of what she saw. The
book is a comic pageant, a panoramic caricature of a small provincial
town. Almost every American town had a Main Street as a matter of
course. Lewis made the name a symbol and an epithet. Main Street
became a synonym for narrow provincialism. People spoke of Main
Street minds or customs without needing to explain further what they
meant. He could have fixed the epithet so deeply in the national consciousness only by giving it the sharp point of unmistakable ideas.
But he reinforced his ideas by innumerable instances. The novel is
full of persons, and they are shown in a continuous variety of incidents to illustrate Gopher Prairie's virtues and vices. The vices seemed
in 1920 to outweigh the virtues overwhelmingly, because they were
shown in a proportion new to American country novels. In time the
vices and virtues came to seem more justly balanced. Much praise
was at first given to the brilliant accuracy of the dialogue. In time it
became clear that the dialogue was partly creation: the American
vernacular enlivened by Lewis's own characteristic idiom and cadences.

A complete example of this enlivened vernacular appeared in his next novel, *Babbitt* (1922), in the speech the hero makes before the Zenith Chamber of Commerce. No actual enthusiast ever spoke with such swift and full and revealing glibness. What Babbitt says is quintessential and archetypal. Thousands of such speeches had been undertaken by such men. Here was the speech they would all have liked to make. Babbitt at once became as much a symbol and an epithet as Main Street, and the name Babbitt a synonym for a conventional business man. From the village Lewis had turned to another American tradition. The business man in fiction had been often a hero, sometimes a malefactor. Lewis studied him more fundamentally, in a case that was taken to be a specimen. George F. Babbitt has not prospered according to the familiar maxims about economy, industry, and perseverance. He has more or less blundered into such success as he has had, in a business which was not his first choice, with a wife whom accident chose for him. He has no thoroughgoing character because he has never needed one. It has been enough for him to do whatever others do, like an indistinguishable bee in an instinctive hive. But in him, as in Carol Kennicott, though not so strongly, there is possibility of dissent. When one of his friends has come to grief by falling out of step, Babbitt reconsiders his own situation. A troubling love affair makes him reflect on his emotional life as he has never done before. Since he has no gift for thinking, and no original opinions, he cannot go far in his little rebellion. In a temporary resentment he struggles to be himself, without quite knowing what his separate self is. And though he soon drops back into the rhythm of the community, he has learned enough to encourage his son in marrying for love and doing the work he likes best. Babbitt's fling has not been pure folly but a kind of abortive triumph.

His triumph was generally overlooked by readers, who failed to notice that this was a classic experience: a man in the midst of prosperity stopping to weigh and value his possessions. The familiar theme was lost in the volume of evidence as to Babbitt's conformity before and after his adventure. Countless critics saw in Babbitt a proof that the typical American was like a standard part of a machine, always ready to be fitted into the national design. It was easy to get such an impression from the book. Lewis had created a whole city in Zenith, the principal town in the synthetic Middle Western state of Winnemac which is impossibly bounded by Michigan, Ohio, Illinois, and Indiana. Gopher Prairie had been a dusty village; Zenith was an enterprising town. Lewis was as much at home in one as in the other. He built the town according to a minute map he had drawn, even to the plans of houses and offices. The many characters besides Babbitt come and go in Zenith with the most convincing naturalness of movement because their lives had all been painstakingly studied. They belong in the town. Their recurrences in the plot confirm the sense that this is the compact community Babbitt feels it to be. Of all Lewis's novels *Babbitt* is the most expertly constructed. Dedicated to Edith Wharton, it made his sprawling Zenith seem as close-knit as her Manhattan, though his vernacular was worlds away from her formal art.

The public expected that after a village and a town Lewis would next write about a large city. He chose not a place but a profession. Grandson, son, nephew, and brother of doctors, he knew the lives of medical families and may have felt, as the sons of American country doctors commonly do, some guilt over not choosing that career himself. There was no current argument about the profession of medicine in which *Arrowsmith* (1925) might take sides. It was the life story of a hero who was successively country doctor, public health official, pathologist in a fashionable clinic, bacteriologist in an institute for medical research, and commissioner sent to fight a plague in the West Indies. The book covers much territory, and it does for an American profession what no other novel has ever done. Carol had been often foolish, Babbitt feeble. Arrowsmith has a more genuine heroism in his passion for scientific integrity. He demandingly looks for it in one grade of his profession after another; when he has despaired of finding it he retires to be a hermit of science in a lonely laboratory in Vermont. There is something Faustian, not to say literary, in Arrowsmith's prayer: "God give me unclouded eyes and freedom from haste. God give me a quiet and relentless anger against all pretense and all pretentious work and all work left slack and unfinished. God give me a restlessness whereby I may neither sleep nor accept praise till my observed results equal my calculated results or in pious glee I discover and assault my error. God give me strength not to trust in God!" There is something true to an honored American tradition in Arrowsmith's retirement. He turns his back on what seem to him worldly confusions and shortsighted compromises, to do his true work in the wilderness, as Daniel Boone and Leather stocking in the eighteenth century had turned away from the settlements which they thought crowded and corrupt. This heroic spirit in Arrowsmith gave fire to his story. But the story itself was far from traditional. It was studied from the most contemporary facts, observed by Lewis himself or derived from the first-hand knowledge of Paul de Kruif, who accompanied Lewis on a cruise to the West Indies for material on tropical conditions. Arrowsmith is more than a simple hero of science. He is very much an individual, divided in will, specific in emotions, generous, charming, and irritating. Leora his first wife is the most convincing and affecting of all Lewis's women, and Gottlieb, Arrowsmith's great teacher, seems actually to be great. The book has memorable episodes, as diverse as the roaring burlesque of the Pickerbaugh campaigns and the pathetic death of Leora. Partly with the help of an admirable presentation on the screen, the story of Arrowsmith became one of the best known of modern American stories, known for its characters and incidents rather than for any such brilliant epithets as Main Street and Babbitt.

Between *Arrowsmith* and his next major novel Lewis published the slighter *Mantrap* (1926), its scene the Canadian woods which he had lately visited, and its satirical object a man blustering about his primitive virtues. Then came *Elmer Gantry* (1927) and controversy again. Gantry is a half-educated, vulgar clergyman who is as much a villain in his profession as Arrowsmith is a hero in his. American fiction had seldom been anti-clerical. When clergymen appeared in it they were likely to be gentle village pastors or robust circuit riders on the frontier or worried ministers with worldly congregations. But the iconoclastic H. L. Mencken, to whom *Elmer Gantry* was dedicated, had for years been pointing out that many settled clergymen were ignorant and intolerant, and that there had grown up a tribe of roving evangelists who were noisy and greedy and sometimes vicious. Lewis studied the type, and other kinds of clergymen, like an anthropologist doing field work. In his life-story of Gantry as student in a small denominational college, as traveling salesman, as manager and lover of a woman evangelist, as ordained minister first in the Baptist then in the Methodist church, driving ahead with unscrupulous ambition to larger and richer charges, Lewis presented his shoddy hero in a full knowledge of the details of such a life. Gantry is a bully, a sneak, a liar, a lecher, a drunkard, and an ignoramus. Lewis was accused of attacking religion, of implying that all clergymen are like Gantry. He was only telling the story of a false priest who himself committed the sins he scourged in others. The book was harsh because Lewis hated the falseness. Nothing decent in Gantry relieves his disgusting story. Without sympathy for him, Lewis gave him a character that was almost all caricature, with sensational and melodramatic coloring.

Again there was a minor book, *The Man Who Knew Coolidge* (1928), a series of monologues by a friend of Babbitt, a leaden treasury of the platitudes he considers to be his own opinions. But in *Dodsworth* (1929) Lewis was only incidentally satirical. Here more profoundly than in any of his novels he studied the ins and outs of a heart through a crucial chapter of a human life. Dodsworth is a Zenith magnate who retires from business. "He would certainly (so the observer assumed) produce excellent motor cars; but he would never love passionately, lose tragically, nor sit in contented idleness upon tropic shores." His story begins as if he were to be another Innocent Abroad, an American taking his humorous ease in Europe. Though Dodsworth values his own country, and often defends it against any kind of censure, he is no brash frontiersman like the Innocents of Mark Twain. That older kind of traveler had passed with the provincial republic of the mid-nineteenth century. But Dodsworth's travels are complicated by his wife, a pampered woman desperately holding on to her youth, fascinated by what seem to her the superior graces of European society, and susceptible to its men. In her bitter discontent she becomes a poisonous shrew, then deserts her husband for a lover. Long in love with her, and long used to cherishing her in spite of her temper, Dodsworth cannot break off either his affection or his sense of responsibility. She is in his blood. The history of his recovery is like a convalescence of a spirit, and it is told with feeling and insight. Externally Dodsworth is the essence of modern America on its grand tour, neither cocksure like Mark Twain's travelers in Europe, nor quivering and colonial like Henry James's. Himself simple, fair-minded, unhappy, he comes in contact with the more extravagant varieties of Americans abroad. The book is a gallery of expatriates. Without either the traditional comedy or the traditional nostalgia of American international novels, *Dodsworth* is a striking study in contrasts. Yet the essence of the book is almost pure drama. Made into a play by Sidney Howard it had a brilliant run on the stage and was equally effective on the screen. After ten years it was the general favorite among Lewis's novels.

In 1930 he was awarded the Nobel Prize in literature, the first American who had received it. His speech of acceptance at Stockholm was a manifesto for the new literature in America, generously naming other writers who might have deserved the honor instead of him. Too few people in his "greatly beloved land," he said, "the most contradictory, the most depressing, the most stirring" country on earth, understood that the United States had "gone through the revolutionary change from rustic colony to world-empire." Too much of its literature was still parochial and timid. Too many of its readers— and writers—were "still afraid of any literature which is not a glorification . . . of our faults as well as our virtues." Its critics and professors of literature too often liked their literature "clear and cold and pure and very dead." But there were "strong young men" who without the support of public standards were "doing such passionate and authentic work that it makes me sick to see that I am a little too old to be one of them. . . . I salute them, with a joy in being not yet too far removed from their determination to give to the America that has mountains and endless prairies, enormous cities and lost far cabins, billions of money and tons of faith, to an America that is as strange as Russia and as complex as China, a literature worthy of her vastness."

It was four years after *Dodsworth,* and the collapse of 1929, before Lewis published another book at all, and six before he once more caught the ground swell of popular opinion. He worked on a novel which was to be about labor in the United States. He could not decide upon a plot. The American labor movement seemed to him to have no form. It was a chaos and tangle of politics full of the conflict of antagonisms which came from Europe. He decided to make his novel perfectly native, the story of three generations of American liberals: a circuit rider on the frontier, a sentimental, heroic socialist, a scientific social engineer. This, Lewis thought, would be his history of a hundred American years. He read a library of books. He drew a magnificent genealogical chart of the family of his first hero, Aaron Gadd. But the story would not take shape in his imagination. More than half of it must run its course in a world of which he could know nothing at first hand. He might by reading find out enough about it for a historian, but not enough for the kind of novelist he was. He gave up the whole enterprise. His *Ann Vickers* (1933) was a full-bodied story of a modern woman in her career, but not Lewis at his best, for the reason that he had not been long or intimately concerned with the material and was not saturated with it. The same defect appeared in *Work of Art* (1934), the story of a hotel-keeper and a procession of hotels.

Seismographic and articulate, Lewis had been more than any other American writer the voice of the liberal decade before 1929. He gave it nation-wide slogans, told it world-wide stories. The depression was confusion for him as well as for his countrymen. The first issue on which he was as clear as in *Main Street* or *Babbitt* was the imperative need of resisting anything like fascism in America. As the dark menace of Hitler rose over Europe it threw an ominous shadow across the Atlantic. All humane men were troubled and apprehensive, but most Americans comforted themselves with the thought that fascism could not reach beyond Europe. Lewis took a common statement for the title of *It Can't Happen Here* (1935). His novel was a prophetic account of what might happen if fascism came to America with the election of a fascist president in the election of 1936. This was only prophecy, which is almost always unsubstantial in fiction, and the details of his forecast seemed at many points copied unconvincingly from events in Nazi Germany. But the book was a tremendous pamphlet, in effect, against tyranny and cruelty, a passionate defense of all that was generous and tolerant in the American way of life. Lewis was taking no position that was novel in him. *Main Street* had been against fascism in the village, *Babbitt* against fascism in business, *Arrowsmith* against fascism in medicine, *Elmer Gantry* against fascism in the ministry. In *It Can't Happen Here* he focused his attention on a possible future in American politics. Countless readers to whom fascism was only a foreign word came to visualize the thing in a native form, ugly and deadly. Made into a play, the story had an unprecedented experience on the stage when the Federal Theater in 1936 produced it with twenty-one companies at the same time throughout the country. For the next three years Lewis devoted himself chiefly to writing for the stage, perhaps, as he believed, learning a new art, and certainly accumulating material for a novel about the theater.

He had become a classic figure in American fiction, and *Arrowsmith* and *Dodsworth* promised to be read by a long posterity. As to the rest of his work, it seemed likely to undergo the same process of selection by time as Mark Twain's had already undergone. The two men had much in common, though Lewis had a better disciplined mind than Mark Twain, and more outspoken courage. Both of them chose large subjects and treated them with high-spirited exuberance. They were fundamentally sensitive and serious, though comedy was for both a natural language. Neither of them excelled in representing women, and neither created memorable lovers, unless the quarreling Dodsworths can be called that. Lewis worked closer to his times than Mark Twain, and produced no such humorous cycle of remembered boyhood as *Tom Sawyer* and *Huckleberry Finn*. Nor did he venture into the past as Mark Twain did in *Joan of Arc* and the *Connecticut Yankee*. Lewis's chief work carried on the kind of examination of the present which Mark Twain began in his *Gilded Age* but did not continue. As this made Lewis the more controversial of the two, and perhaps the more temporary, it also involved him more deeply in living issues. The living issues of one age have a way of living on into another. There can be no question that his books are landmarks in the history of American opinions through two crucial decades. Yet when these opinions come to seem no longer so pressing, the characters who held them will still seem alive because they held them so passionately. The imagined city of Zenith will still have its firm place on the map of the American imagination, Babbitt in Zenith will run through his little year of discontent and turn back to a sorry grace. Arrowsmith, studying medicine at the university a few miles away, will find Leora in a Zenith hospital. Elmer Gantry will carry on his loud crusades in Zenith. Dodsworth, when his peace has been broken and healed in Europe, will think of Zenith as his home. Side by side with actual Middle Western cities, Zenith has appeared to be pure nature. But Zenith is art. When the actual cities have faded or changed, Zenith, with all its crude colors and satiric drawing, will stand up like a monument. A comic energy like Lewis's has a lasting as well as a compelling power.

# Martin Arrowsmith and His Habitat

## by T. R. Fyvel

Sinclair Lewis we find it harder and harder to believe we could ever have taken for a serious writer. The figure of Babbitt remains in our mind, a caricature of attitude to which we no longer respond; but Lewis himself we remember as a cartoonist, a journalist with neither poetic nor psychological depth. . . .

I feel that this categorical judgment by Mr. Leslie Fiedler probably represents the view of many present-day critics. Yet I think it does not explain the phenomenon of Lewis' immense popularity thirty years ago. In a way it evades this phenomenon. And as I sat down to reread *Arrowsmith,* at first almost like a boys' book and then with growing fascination, I felt more and more that Lewis as novelist still awaits his reassessment.

Of course, the fascination of reading *Arrowsmith* was rather like that of watching the jerks of an old, revived silent film. As Mr. Maxwell Geismar has pointed out, Lewis' earlier books are as much romances as satires. In rereading *Arrowsmith* one is immediately struck by this romantic note. Indeed, the whole construction of the book is romantically schematic. Martin as a boy is first seen as a restless-eyed youngster who skips the games with the Gang because he is fascinated by old Doc Vickerson's consultation room and its apparatus; and he never leaves this pose till the end of the story. For Martin is America; or at least he is the seeker after truth in the United States of the early twentieth century. As a poor but passionate medical student at Winnemac, near Zenith, he is saved from fateful involvement with a literary lady by marriage with Leora Tozer, a fellow-rebel from the Midwest. He is irrevocably directed toward research by his encounter with Max Gottlieb, a saturnine, exiled German-Jewish professor, who may be socially innocent but represents scientific integrity at its highest level. So the stage is set, and from now on Martin fights for scientific research and the soul of America.

*"Martin Arrowsmith and His Habitat" by T. R. Fyvel. From* The New Republic, *CXXXIII (July 18, 1955), 16-18. Reprinted by permission of* The New Republic, © *1955, Harrison-Blaine of New Jersey, Inc.*

As a young doctor in a small, dreary Dakota prairie town, Martin loses his first practice through erratic and quixotic behavior in defense of truth. Talent, however, cannot be denied: Martin is shot up to his next job of Public Health Officer in Nautilus, a Midwest Middletown. Again defending science and truth against local politics, Martin again loses out—and once more moves up, this time to Chicago, to a job as pathologist in a smooth, wealthy Chicago surgical clinic. Then research calls through the person of Max Gottlieb, and Martin now moves to the famous McGurk Institute of Research in Manhattan. But even here at the summit, as the current phrase would have it, Martin finds science and truth beset by social and commercial falsehoods against which he flings himself into battle. And this battle continues unchecked, even after Martin has become famous, after the faithful Leora has died, after he has climbed the social heights of Manhattan by a second marriage. At the end of the book Martin is shown in a romantic spotlight. He has again walked out on a lush social life and is living rough in an up-state shack where he and a fellow-scientist will carry on research. Dr. Arrowsmith is, in fact, back where the boy Martin started out. In the theme of the fairy story there is no development.

The style in which this story is told is also as much a romantic as a journalistic one. The impression is often not only of slang which is outdated, but of outdated slang which never quite existed except for the author himself. Thus Martin gloats, hungers, rejoices, rages, snorts, stalks, glowers, smarts, frets and snarls his way through the book. He speaks in pregnant shorthand: "Dakota. Real man's country. Frontier. Opportunity. America." Among stylistic infelicities, the following is probably a fair sample. Martin's wealthy second wife has just given birth to a son they have called John:

> They did not know it, but a certain John Arrowsmith, mariner of Bideford, had died in the matter of the Spanish Armada, taking with him five valorous dons.
>
> Joyce suffered horribly and renewed all of Martin's love for her (he did love pitifully this slim, brilliant girl).
>
> "Death's a better game than bridge—you have no partner to help you!" she said, when she was grotesquely stretched on a chair of torture and indignity. . . .

Each of the theree sentences here has its embarrassing note: in the first it is the schoolboy reference to the Armada and the "five valorous dons"; in the second, the combination of "pitifully" and "this slim, brilliant girl"; in the third, the use of bridge, then evidently still a novel game, as the symbol of an upper-class flirtation with death.

So much for the deficiencies of *Arrowsmith*. I feel they might strike a reader of the nineteen-fifties almost at the first glance, especially a critic in search of truly serious literature. Yet as one looks again closely at the pages, the qualities which gave Lewis his immense impact still stand out. There is first of all the immense zest—the zest not merely of an extravagant personality, but of a whole age; let's say the age when even American vulgarity was still politically innocent. Then there is the effectiveness of much of the caricature. Take the proper names: what better name could be given an American craftsman of science, descended from a Devon mariner, than "Martin Arrowsmith"? Martin's fellow-student with suspect religious mania and odors is called the Reverend Ira Hinkley. Martin's vulgarian of a chief in the Public Health Department is Almus Pickerbaugh. The sleek socialite director of the McGurk Institute is Dr. Rippleton Holabird, while the rough biochemist who rescues Martin for the simple life is Terry Wickett. An obvious technique; yet I found these names had over the years remained half-familiar to me, like the lines of an effective cartoon. This may well have been their purpose. As Mr. Fiedler observed in his stricture, Lewis was essentially a cartoonist; and if his work is judged in this light, he may come out quite well indeed.

For the point about any good cartoonist is that he must work from a private nightmare vision, but one so controlled that it can find expression within a rigid and narrow frame. And in Lewis' early work one can find such a nightmare clearly indicated, perhaps most vividly in *Babbitt,* but also in *Arrowsmith*.

There is the rigid narrowness of range. In his novels Lewis has really only one subject or, one might almost say, one character. This was the thriving, philistine middle-class society of the Middle West from which he sprang. Early in the twentiest century the wheels of American capitalism were turning steadily, and this society was being rapidly transformed. In *Babbitt,* Lewis gave his own impression of the new hectic American capitalist life. It is important to recognize this impression as nightmarish. On the one side you have the incessant bustle of Zenith, the zip city, with its office towers and automobiles and golf courses and gadgets; you have Babbitt and his fellow businessmen continuously growing richer or hoping to grow richer. But in fact the Zenith scene is demonic. It is a world not only of non-art and non-culture, but also of of non-security and non-love. Because for Babbitt and his colleagues, there is no let-up. They seem to live on the sufferance of unknown financial forces. Let Babbitt make $15,000 or $25,000 a year: one false step will still be enough to bring ruin. They have as good as no family relationships to lean on, and there is no hope for non-conformity. In fact, as Mr.

Geismar has mentioned, Lewis' characters closely observed, end up
by seeming to belong to a strange class . . .

> . . . a middle class which is essentially without a home life, without
> children, without religion, and finally, without an economic status to
> speak of: a middle class which is without all the historic props of a
> middle class.

Nor is there a way out from this world of demonic middle-class
competition. Neither aristocracy nor workers are more than vaguely
sketched in. The world of the Zenith Athletic Club with its grimaces
and forced jokes, is in fact that of a Sartrian hell.

Against this background Lewis draws his leading characters, and it
seems, again, part of the nightmare that they should be utterly
solitary. Thus, in *Main Street,* Carol Kennicott must wage a one-
woman struggle against all Gopher Prairie. George F. Babbitt to be
sure may seem to live amidst that perpetual din of other realtors and
boosters. But Lewis is at pains to stress Babbitt's malaise, that Babbitt's
all-electric house suffered from the defect "that it was not a home,"
that Babbitt's intimate relations with his wife Myra were long dead,
that he was hardly conscious of his children and that his attempt
to maintain one genuine friendship with his "Paulibus" has to end
in disaster. And similarly, in *Arrowsmith,* Lewis writes laconically
on page four: "Martin's father and mother were dead, leaving him
only enough money for his art and medical courses." Having no
family or background Martin can also be left conveniently without
any (non-scientific) individual traits; nor does he pick up any such
through the book. If Lewis at the close momentarily provides Martin
with a second wife who has a secure social position and even bears
Martin a son, he quickly lets Martin escape and even express fear
of this son, a minuscule aristocrat, that is, a non-middle-class figure.

In fact, the psychological struggle described by Lewis in the early
books is unchanging; on the one side a demonic American society
from which there is no escape, on the other side a hero or heroine
whose solitariness is complete. It has been said against Lewis that
these struggles take place in a harsh, unvarying daylight illumination,
without nuances. True, this absence of nuances is a literary deficiency.
But is it not also part of Lewis' private nightmare, and therefore of
his strength and rigidity as a cartoonist?

After all, the same charge, that he could smell out social trends but
not draw living individual characters, could also be fairly put against
George Orwell. And the answer could be given that like Lewis, Orwell
was so preoccupied with describing his social nightmare that he had
little attention left for subtle individual characters. Indeed, given the
difference of a generation, and of course of creative power, quite a

few parallels can be drawn between Lewis' Zenith and Orwell's Airstrip One. Against George Babbitt's unsuccessful attempt to buck the system of Zenith middle-class society, one can set Winston Smith's doomed revolt against the Party. One is merely a development of the other. And can the reflection of Hiroshima not be glimpsed on the nightmare horizon of cultureless Zenith?

All this may seem far-fetched. But the point is that Lewis' weakness lay not in his cartoonist's technique—why shouldn't he be a cartoonist —nor his stand as social critic, but in his failure ever to develop his methods of social criticism beyond their starting point. Of course he had his emotional ambivalence, too. As his sneers against the literary characters he includes in his books indicate, the American middle class was as much a society he ultimately loved as the target for his anger. At any rate, even as the Depression hit American capitalism, Lewis seemed ready to make his peace with it. And in this shift of attitude, *Arrowsmith* occupies the key position. Two years earlier, with *Babbitt,* Lewis had reached his height as a satirical cartoonist and said all he could say about America. His task was performed. In *Arrowsmith* he did not actually retreat—not as yet. If one looks carefully, one can see that in this novel a complete balance is maintained in the struggle between a destructive society and the solitary hero. Each time that the forces of American careerism, vulgarity and money-grubbing pull Martin down, his genius enables him to rise back to a better position; but each advantage he gains is in turn snatched from him.

So at the end the issue is left undecided: perhaps this balanced novel was meant to be a portrait in a mirror. At any rate, after *Arrowsmith* the balance tilted away from Lewis' nightmare, and hence away from his focus as cartoonist. In *Elmer Gantry,* which followed, he hit out only at stage dummies. And in his pictures of *Dodsworth,* the Zenith middle-class aristocrat, and *Ann Vickers,* the social reformer, he was already trying to achieve a compromise between his chief characters and the formerly demonic social scene. Of the books which followed after these two little need be said. One need only compare Lewis' *It Can't Happen Here* with the writings of Orwell and Koestler to realize how little his ideas had developed in the era which followed the crash of 1929.

And yet, let us again be fair. What if this was *not* Lewis' era any longer? What if his lack of intellectual development lay inherent in his original nightmare: did this nightmare not also provide him with the creative obsession and cartoonist's technique which produced *Main Street, Babbitt* and *Arrowsmith?* In those three books, at any rate, Lewis captured a glimpse of an American age: which remains in all conscience a serious enough feat for a writer.

## PART TWO

## View Points

## Anon., *Times Literary Supplement*: *Martin Arrowsmith**

There is a stirring epic quality in Mr. Sinclair Lewis's new novel. "Martin Arrowsmith" is easily the best work he has yet given us. Mr. Lewis's observation is here strengthened by a vision less parochial than that which contributed to the novelty of "Main Street" or "Babbitt." In "Martin Arrowsmith" he has attempted a far less obvious criticism of society than the mere indictment of dullness and prejudice; and, as a consequence, his analysis goes very near the psychological roots of social idealism. This it does by projecting the individual aims and outlook of the scientist below the surface of organized social effort. The serious intention entails no loss of imaginative interest. The constant and unrelenting pursuit of truth, even of truth that does no more than deny belief and assail unproven speculation, is the occupation of a hero; and Martin brings to the religion of a scientist all the heroic virtues and shortcomings. As a human being he is only an uncommon mixture of idealism and egotism, a saintly adventurer and a monster of intolerance; as a bacteriologist he is anointed with the oil of the chosen of God.

Into his history is cast the ambition and urgency of the modern scientific consciousness. He is first and foremost the protagonist in the drama of human knowledge and power, and only afterwards the untutored and zealous devotee of life. Leora, the warm, vulgar, wise barbarian who loves him, submits to Martin because, as she tells him, "your work is more important to you than I am, maybe more important than you are." But others will neither love nor submit with such keen faith; and in the common and essential tasks of the hour the seeker is torn between human interests and the worship of truth. He may believe that truth is no more than a sceptical attitude to life and despair of the unattainable finality to which hope alone is led, but, in the ecstasy of cold, unchallengeable discovery, his recognition of scientific law places him beyond the sovereignty of fear and questioning. If Martin is to acknowledge the passion of his quest he must ulti-

"Martin Arrowsmith." *From* Times Literary Supplement, *XXIV (March 5, 1925),* *153. Copyright 1925 by the London* Times. *Reprinted by permission of the* *publisher. An ellipsis indicates the omission of a portion of the original text.*

* This was the title under which the novel was published, by Jonathan Cape, Ltd., in England. [R.J.G.]

mately renounce the pleasant and comfortable ties which bind him to the world of virtue, kindliness, merit, and obligation. He must continue to seek the hidden and uncharted order of life in the domain of medical science, sacrificing, if needs be, all other satisfactions to the terrible glory of truth and law. . . .

We have spoken so far only of the intellectual content of the novel. For its sincere emotion, insight, gaiety, and general artistry we have as unreserved a respect. Perhaps the tale is occasionally episodic and a shade too detailed, but it is rich in understanding, brimming with fun, with a troubled humour that does not obscure silent but intense indignation, touched with profound pity for the loneliness of the true explorer. Mr. Lewis is sensitive to both the shames and the exaltations of the scientist. Viewing his aspiration, he is appalled by the waste and folly of social tyranny, scornful of the complacent ignorance and suspicion of the mob. So far as Martin's ideals for science are concerned, there is little difference between the attitude of the millions in New York and the attitude of the few hundred people living in Main Street of Wheatsylvania, in North Dakota. The same dreary hypocrisy, stubborn stupidity, herd instincts, coarse materialism, and sentimental indulgence that went to the making of a thousand Babbitts in Zenith—George F. appears for a moment in the story—follow Martin as a student at the University of Winnemac, as a doctor in Nautilus, even as a research worker in the proudest city of the United States. But the seeds of faith were sown at Winnemac. The magnificent patience and visionary ardour of Max Gottlieb claimed Martin for science, for a passion that neither bargained nor made conditions, for a quest that should be its own reward. And Leora's generosity of spirit held him to his undertaking. If Martin is the hero of Mr. Lewis's novel, Gottlieb and Leora must be reckoned the inspiration of his heroism. The three characters are probably as real as it is possible for the written word to make them. And Leora's death on the plague-stricken island, Gottlieb's living death, and the awkward, mute friendship between Martin and Terry stamp themselves on the mind with the force of personal memories.

## H. L. Mencken: *Arrowsmith*

Of Sinclair Lewis' technical skill it is unnecessary to speak. The fellow, indeed, has a vast cunning at the art he adorns and staggers—

*"Arrowsmith" by H. L. Mencken. From* American Mercury, *IV, (April, 1925), 507-509. Copyright 1925 by* American Mercury. *Reprinted by permission of the editor, LaVonne D. Furr, Torrance, Calif. Ellipses indicate the omission of portions of the original text.*

far more than any of the high-toned English novelists who swarm across the ocean to instruct and patronize Yankee blighters. If he would pull himself together, translate his very sure instincts into plain propositions, and put them on paper, the result would be the best treatise on novel-writing ever heard of. His "Babbitt" is not only an extremely engaging story, full of grotesque and devastating humors; it is also, in structure, the very model of a modern novel. It hangs together admirably. It moves, breathes, lives. From the first page to the last there is not the slightest faltering in direction or purpose. . . . Even in "Main Street," vast in area, crowded with people and flabby in design, he never got lost for an instant. And even in "Arrowsmith," treading unfamiliar and arduous ground and constantly confronted by technical problems of a complicated and onerous sort, he never wobbles. Once the thing gets under way—and it gets under way toward the bottom of the first page—it thunders on in a straight line to an inescapable conclusion. There are episodes, true enough. There is what the musicians call passage work. There are moments of voluptuous lingering, as over stuff too sweet to be left behind. But there is never any uncertainty in design. There is never any wavering in theme or purpose.

That theme, in brief, is the burden which lies upon any man, in our highly materialistic society, who gives over his life to the pursuit of truth—not only the indifference and contempt which he must face, but also the positive opposition which he must face. The public theory, of course, is that the tide runs the other way. Haven't we two or three hundred universities, more than all Europe and all Asia, and don't all of them devote at least a part of their funds to keeping scholars? Aren't there scores of great foundations for research, maintained gloriously by Baptists in the oil business, Rotarians in the chewing tobacco business, Harvard graduates in the bond business? Doesn't the government itself provide three thousand jobs for scientists? Are not thousands more employed by the States, the cities, the correspondence schools, the rolling mills, the manufacturers of vaccines, tooth-pastes, oleomargarine, sheep washes, wall-papers, ready-mixed paints? All true, and yet the tragic fact remains. What ails every one of these undertakings for the fostering of science is that, whatever its pretensions on the label, it is utilitarian in the bottle—that its primary aim is to back the scientist into a comfortable stall and milk him like a cow. . . .

Yet scientists remain among us. They are hatched every year, sometimes in low life. The passion which animated Johannes Müller and Karl Ludwig penetrates, curiously, to the remotest reaches of the land. Of our two native-born Nobel prize-winners—both workers in pure science—one was born in an Illinois village and the other in a suburb of Philadelphia. But what is the national machinery for rescuing such fellows from their surroundings, and helping them to develop their powers? Is it effective? Does it work? The thesis of "Arrowsmith" is that it doesn't—that, on the contrary, it opposes and hobbles them— that most of its help goes to quacks. Nearly five hundred pages are devoted to that thesis—five hundred pages of riotous and often barbarous humor, yet always with a sharp undertone of irony in it, always with a bitter flavor. Lewis, in brief, preaches. Well, if this be preaching let us have more of it! For it has the strange aim, for preaching, of combating fraud and obscurantism, of getting at and hymning the truth. It has a moral, but there is in it no snuffling moralizing. Arrowsmith is no peerless Florestan, standing against the Philistines. He shares all their weaknesses. He is almost as bad as they are—but not quite. In the end, after long and dreadful battles, some ending with his defeat outright and some with his surrender, he escapes by flight. So "science" goes marching on, its banners flying, Babbitts clearing the way, a mule-load of gold every ten paces. And Martin, saved at last, woos science-without-the-quotation-marks in his austere retreat, rid at last of all urging to get "practical" results.

The book has interested me immensely. It is well thought out and executed with great skill. . . . Pickerbaugh exists everywhere, in almost every American town. He is the quack who flings himself melodramatically upon measles, chicken pox, whooping cough—the organizer of Health Weeks and author of prophylactic, Kiwanian slogans —the hero of clean-up campaigns—the scientific beau ideal of newspaper reporters, Y.M.C.A. secretaries, and the pastors of suburban churches. He has been leering at the novelists of America for years, and yet Lewis and De Kruif were the first to see and hail him. They have made an almost epic figure of him. He is the Babbitt of this book—far more charming than Arrowsmith himself, and far more real. Arrowsmith fails in one important particular: he is not typical, he is not a good American. I daresay that many a reader, following his struggles with the seekers for "practical" results, will sympathize frankly with the latter. After all, it is not American to prefer honor to honors; no man, pursuing that folly, could ever hope to be president of the United States. Pickerbaugh will cause no such lifting of eyebrows. Like Babbitt, he will be recognized instantly and enjoyed innocently. Within six weeks, I suspect, every health officer in America will be receiving letters denouncing him as a Pickerbaugh. Thus nature imitates art.

## Robert Morss Lovett: An Interpreter of American Life

Mr. Sinclair Lewis, like Mr. H. L. Mencken, is a paradox in the United States today. A leading trait of the American people is a youthful self-consciousness amounting to an inferiority complex, which makes us impatient of all criticism. Everything which we have done is right because we did it. All our wars were just; all our statesmen are pure; all our business is honest. Ours is the land of liberty, of tolerance, of opportunity, of righteousness. Our favourite prophets are the sayers of smooth things in Zion, those who speak comfortably to Jerusalem of her ideals and performances—Wilson, Harding, Coolidge. And yet by some sort of saving grace, in the midst of this complacency appear Mr. Lewis and Mr. Mencken, to tear the hoods and sheets off our moral and civic Ku Klux Klan, to show the cringing forms and the false, cowardly, cruel faces beneath the mask—and Mr. Mencken and Mr. Lewis as critic and novelist are, in this day and generation, the most read and considered interpreters of American life. They are constantly telling truths about their country for which less fortunate devils are being hounded out of pulpits and college chairs, losing business and social standing, and occasionally suffering physical punishment at the hands of court or clan, and yet they flourish like two green bay trees.

One explanation of this phenomenon is to be found in the fact that both Mr. Mencken and Mr. Lewis write the American language. It is a natural impulse when one hears one's own tongue in the midst of foreign speech—and most of his literature is foreign to the ordinary sensual American—to turn and listen, even if the meaning is unpleasant. And a second explanation lies in the fact that both Mr. Mencken and Mr. Lewis are good-natured and affable. They find the spectacle one tending to amusement rather than indignation. Humour is the form in which the American takes his cathartic—the Biglow Papers, Josh Billings, Artemus Ward, and Mark Twain, for examples. Even so there is still an unexplainable residuum, especially in the case of Mr. Lewis who is undoubtedly long and, in the opinion of many readers whose devotion is the more remarkable, dull. If Mr. Lewis attracts his great audience by the sense of reality which his pages convey, and the careless humour of his approach, he holds it by a sense of the importance of what he has to say.

In Main Street Mr. Lewis employed the inclusive formula of the

"*An Interpreter of American Life*" by Robert Morss Lovett. From The Dial, LXXVIII (June, 1925), 515-18. Ellipses indicate the omission of portions of the original text.

naturalists, setting down as much of the visual and audible stuff of life in Gopher Prairie as his vehicle could carry, the motive power being furnished by the ambitions of Carol Kennicott, wife of the local physician. In Babbitt he adopted a much more rapid and impressionistic method. The life of Zenith is merely the background for the hero, who in his egregious vulgarity and pitiful self-conceit, is accepted everywhere along with General Dawes as the typical American business man, booster, and patrioteer. If Main Street looks back to Zola, Babbitt is in the more humorous, highly coloured, exaggerated manner of Daudet. George F. Babbitt is an American Tartarin. In Arrowsmith, Mr. Lewis returns to his earlier method. There is much of life as it is lived in a Mid-Western university town, a Dakota village, an Iowa city, and finally in New York; but the background is chiefly occupational. Martin Arrowsmith is a physician and a medical scientist, and the experience of his disillusionment with that high calling is the core of the book. . . .

In all this [experience] there is something of the conscientious thoroughness of Zola. Mr. Lewis is determined to leave no stone of the medical edifice unturned, and under each he finds human nature in reptilian form. Indeed, to reach the fraud of the commercial drug firm he is obliged to cut loose from the hero and follow the story of his teacher, Professor Gottlieb, on his way from Winnemac to McGurk. Undoubtedly in this occupational interest we miss something of the regional unity of Main Street and Babbitt. We do not know Mohalis, Wheatsylvania, and Nautilus as we do Gopher Prairie and Zenith. Toward the end of the book the social background of New York is hardly realized at all, and this is the chief reason why its entrance into Arrowsmith's life with his second marriage seems mere fiction. The essential truth of Arrowsmith's experience as medical student, country doctor, and director of public health, no physician will question. Even the preposterous Pickerbaugh, Director of Public Health of Nautilus, Iowa, is plausible enough to readers in New York and Chicago. Pickerbaugh revives the exuberant caricature of Babbitt, . . . [which] is in Mr. Lewis's best vein. When he conducts Arrowsmith to the McGurk laboratory we feel that he is on less firm ground. Here he is indebted to Dr. Paul H. De Kruif for the inside stuff. The bacteriological detail is, of course, sound. Never before in fiction has the psychology of the scientist, the passion for research, been rendered with such penetration and justice. When, however, Arrowsmith in fighting the plague in St. Hubert is bidden by his scientific conscience to divide the population into two parts, one half to be inoculated with his phage, the other half to be refused in order absolutely to control the results of the experiment, we have either an example of scientific fanaticism or a piece of pure fiction. The phenomena of the plague have been sufficiently observed to make it practically certain that, if all who were inoculated under favourable circumstances survived, the remedy had been found—and probably half the population would have resisted inoculation anyway. This air of unreality hangs over the latter part of the book as Mr. Lewis becomes more absorbed in his purpose. . . .

Arrowsmith is an important step in the campaign to de-bamboozle the American public and relieve its institutions of bunk. Mr. Lewis has attacked this old enemy in one of its highest places. In all phases of medicine—education, private and public practice, and finally research—he has revealed its pretensions and exposed its perpetrators. If he has sacrificed the reality of fiction, it is in the interest of the reality of a public cause which gives largeness of view and significance to Arrowsmith.

## *Joseph Wood Krutch*: A Genius on Main Street

It might have been reasonably objected against Mr. Sinclair Lewis that in his two pictures of mediocrity triumphant he failed to recognize one important fact. In spite of all the optimism which lay behind his satires he made his heroes succumb with surprising ease to the dullness which surrounded them, and he seemed never to be aware of that almost magical sureness with which something born in the natural artist or in the natural scientist enables him to seek and find the best in the most unlikely places. By a sort of intuition such a man divines the existence of the things which he has never learned; he goes straight to the best books without ever being told their names; and he recognizes naturally the best by virtue of a taste which has never been cultivated. He may, if his environment has been too unfortunate, bear always certain scars or even suffer certain deformities; but he will never like Carol surrender absolutely to Main Street or like Babbitt wholly lose himself if he began with any talent sufficiently robust to be significant.

Doubtless it was not so intended, but Mr. Lewis's new novel might serve as an answer to the objections just raised, for it is the story of a man who managed, by virtue of his intuitions, to win a partial triumph over those forces before which the author's other heroes went down in defeat. Martin Arrowsmith was born in as hopeless a town as Mr. Lewis ever conceived, and he got his first ideas of medicine from a drunken failure; but by virtue of that insight of which I have spoken

*"A Genius on Main Street" by Joseph Wood Krutch. From* The Nation, *CXX (April 1, 1925), 359-360. Copyright 1925 by* The Nation. *Reprinted by permission of the editor.*

he recognized perfection instead of imperfection and guessed rather than learned what a scientist in medicine should be. By that bit of magical insight he proved that he had in him the talent which counts, and the rest of his life was of a piece with his beginning. He went to a medical school which was noisier and more vulgar than most; he established his practice in a Main Street town and he served on the Main Street board of health; he was even exposed to the more subtle blandishments of the commercialized research foundation; but he never failed to see or to guess the realities which were behind the sham. Thus Mr. Lewis has formulated once more his indictment of American civilization, but he has made it more convincing than it ever was before because he has, in a sense, made it less absolute. He has described once more, with that wealth of documentation and that concrete actuality so peculiarly his, the difficulties which beset the idealist; but he has qualified his thesis by saying, in effect, that these difficulties are not absolutely insurmountable, and this means, in a word, that he has chosen a more important hero than he has ever chosen before. If American society lost in Carol and in Mr. Babbitt two tolerable human beings and got in return two monstrosities, the fact is not, perhaps, extremely important; but the fact that Martin Arrowsmith was, obviously, not quite what he might have been is a very important fact indeed.

Fundamentally Mr. Lewis has only one theme. All of his characters from Mr. Wren to Arrowsmith are alike in that the dominant desire, conscious or unconscious, of each is the desire for that complete life which has not been afforded him, and the burden of each novel is the difficulty of finding such a life in barbarous America. He has shown in two books what happens to mediocrity in such an environment; he shows now what the same environment can do to a man who is very near a genius. In the early pages of the present novel he describes his hero, still a medical student, planning his career while he eats his lunch—an enormous banana split with a bar of chocolate—and never, I think, has he given a more typical picture of one of the characteristically grotesque aspects of our civilization or better summed up, by implication, his criticism of it. One may suitably plan one's life in the midst of many different environments, in the depths of a primeval forest or in the attic of an ancient city, in the library of a venerable institution or even in a German beer garden; but one cannot possibly plan it on the stool of a soda fountain in the midst of banana splits without running the very grave risk that something of the barbarous ugliness of the place and something of the sticky un-wholesomeness of the diet may corrupt that life. There is nothing immoral about a soda fountain, but there is about it something fundamentally ugly and ridiculous, and America, so Mr. Lewis says, is a land of soda fountains, a land which provides no suitable background, physical or spiritual, for the cultivation of life. A little later Martin, taken to hear a casual concert of German music, is incomprehensibly stirred and his vague longings take shape around the personality of an instructor in bacteriology who happens to be the only product he knows of the completer civilization which he guesses. "He exulted, 'I am going to have 'em all—the fame of Max Gottlieb—I mean his ability—and the lovely music and the lovely women—golly! I am going to do big things. And see the world . . . will this piece never quit?' " It is once more a complete description of Mr. Lewis's vision of America and a summary of all that he has to say—that we are a nation eager for that rich and complete life which includes a good deal more than what is commonly called culture and which Martin Arrowsmith, like most of his fellow-countrymen, never achieved because, in spite of his integrity and his genuine successes in science, he was compelled to grow up in a relatively barren soil.

"Arrowsmith" will probably not attract the enormous attention which "Main Street" and "Babbitt" attracted because it is not so remarkable as a pamphlet; but considered purely as a novel it is better than either because it has a more striking fable and because it is essentially truer.

## *Haven Emerson, M.D.*: A Doctor Looks at Arrowsmith

All medical students will of course read Sinclair Lewis' latest, some physicians too; and these will be interested because of the simulacra of medical personalities so thinly veiled in the story of Martin Arrowsmith, village doctor's drudge, crude student of the dull Middle West, aimless crossroads practitioner, health adventurer, spasmodic laboratory searcher and finally, sans selfrespect and wanting even affection, the sham recluse, husband of a lion-hunting social dodder.

Certainly this story was not written for the entertainment or inspiration of doctors, nor to carry a lesson or promote a cause. Built for the laity, assembled, we are to believe, from family traditions of earlier Lewis practitioners, and by the aid of an intensive association with a present day doctor of philosophy, this story may be judged as a work of art, or by its effect upon those human relationships which the applied sciences have fostered in the home under the persuasion of the hand and word of doctors of medicine.

"A Doctor Looks at Arrowsmith" by Haven Emerson, M.D. From **The Survey,** LIV (May 1, 1925), 180. Copyright 1925 by **The** Survey. Reprinted by permission of Ethel Emerson Wortis.

Real interest is maintained throughout; but the boy or girl who thinks of medicine as a career must have a strong stomach, and a keen loyalty to his own clear vision, to persist through college, hospital and the fickle fortunes of private practice, with such a sordid picture before him, unrelieved by anything sweet and wholly true except the clear soul of Leora, so brave a sweetheart, so wise a wife.

The satire is stinging, deserved perhaps. Yet like so many of the misbegotten daubs offered by painters as interpretations of their own distorted emotions and crude mentalities, what might have been a rare realistic novel has suffered from the same lack of proportion and excursions into extravaganza that make of the daily press a school of literary pathology. Flashes of fine service, glimpses of gallant deeds, shrewd skill, clean courage, and now and then a redeeming reckless-ness serve to carry one over sodden pages of booze and selfishness. Health officers and other promoters of those buffoonery weeks of hocus-pocus hygiene will rejoice in the picturesque abstract from the life of Pickerbaugh, who shares with Leora the best skill of the author.

We see but too brightly American medicine as it might have been if there had been lacking background, sincerity or any of those ele-ments which have pulled it through and past and beyond the sorry makeshifts of the tobacco-chewing era of corn-tassel colleges.

From an author of such ability we could wish a more typical doctor for his hero. What would Arrowsmith have done if his own dull neglect of his precious trusting Dakota bride had not denied her the career of mother? Where would his poker and his intermittent drunks have led him if he had given a mere man's usual hostages and been bound to labor by the burden of a family? Elders and little children are too common a cause for stability, of urgent necessity for earning, to be so wholly ignored in this cartoon of a classical human career.

We have a cast of pitiful pawns, students, teachers, practitioners of medicine and health! Shall we believe it or suspect that Sinclair Lewis and his arbiter laboratoriorum, De Kruif, have seen less of the Hesse-links, or were perhaps less interested in them than in the wide variety of cheap and costly crooks they so elaborate upon in Arrowsmith's career. Much amusement, many sneers, plenty of comparisons with known nonentities will follow in the wake of such a reading. What more?

One could wish for some high hope, and sweet purpose in life to come of any story of one's countrymen, of one's professional fellows. How can author or publisher justify so much trouble in digging up typical tales of sorry folk all over the land, when poverty of spirit is so commonplace as to be unworthy of this abundant gossip?

## W. P. K.: *Martin Arrowsmith*

It is not often that a novel calls for review in a scientific journal, but Mr. Sinclair Lewis has given us in *Martin Arrowsmith* a work of such interest and importance that notice of it should not be neglected. It is a long novel dealing with the life problem of a young medical student and practitioner in the United States, who is handicapped by the common difficulty of narrow financial straits. He is inspired by the fine fire that consumes the true research worker to the exclusion of all else, and perpetually has to fight his superiors, who demand practical results and cannot see the importance of fundamental research *per se*. If the book brings home to any of the public the force of this idea, as it surely must, then it will do a very great service to research.

The other characters are remarkably well drawn, and though the "two-fisted fighting poet Doc" Pickerbaugh, of a State Public Health Service, may appear somewhat of a caricature to British eyes, doubtless he has his prototypes in the newer civilisation of America. Max Gottlieb, the bacteriologist, is excellent, and his gospel of truth so well set out that it should be an inspiration to many others who choose the hard paths of research as it was to Martin Arrowsmith.

What is called the "human interest" is not neglected, but we can see that Mr. Lewis was much more interested in the relation of Martin's emotional life to his work than to the mere story of it; viewed only as a tale, however, it makes excellent reading.

In a preliminary note, the author acknowledges the help of Dr. Paul de Kruif afforded him with the medical parts of the work, and with his scientific philosophy, and we can only say we should be glad to meet this gentleman. Mr. Lewis showed great promise in his earlier work, but here he has surely found himself, and we have no hesitation in strongly recommending this book to all research workers.

"Martin Arrowsmith." *From* Nature, *CXV* (*May 23, 1925*), *797. Copyright 1925 by Macmillan & Co. Ltd. Reprinted by permission of the publisher.* "*W. P. K.*" *has been identified by the present editors of* Nature *as W. P. Kennedy, but no further information could be obtained.*

## *Edwin Muir*: Melodrama in America

If we are to believe Mr. Sinclair Lewis, science is, like big business, a very melodramatic affair in America. In it, as in finance, social re-

"Melodrama in America" *by Edwin Muir. From an omnibus review of current novels in* The Nation & The Athenaeum, *XXXVI* (*March 14, 1925*), *818. Copyright 1925 by* The Nation & The Athenaeum. *Reprinted by permission of* The New Statesman.

form, and religion, there is unfair competition, hustling, boosting; and the scientist who stops to verify a discovery before he makes it public is looked down upon. In "Martin Arrowsmith" Mr. Lewis tries to do for American science what he did in "Babbitt" for American business life; but though he is as incisive as ever, the theme does not give him much scope. It is not convincing, simply because the public prejudices of a people, or even of popular scientists, can do nothing finally against the discovery of new truths, which is the real business of science. Science can hardly be made a social problem, and one feels that Mr. Lewis's reforming zeal has misled him. There is, however, some very effective satire in the book on all sorts of shams and illiberalities. . . .

## *Henry Seidel Canby*: Fighting Success

With "Arrowsmith" Sinclair Lewis justifies and achieves his ambition to become a national novelist. Manifest destiny has been the watchword of this nation, and Success the chief objective of its inhabitants. In two remarkable stories, "Main Street" and "Babbitt," Mr. Lewis has satirically pursued in the characters of his heroes common ideals of American success and proved them failure. Main Street, as Lewis sees it, is failure, and so is Carol Kennicott; Zenith is failure —spiritually and emotionally failure—and so is the rather pathetic Babbitt. And now Lewis drives home his moral by choosing for protagonist a very human scientist congenitally opposed to success as America sees success, a scientist meshed and intermeshed in a social organization made to achieve success, fighting it, fought by it, triumphing by seizing in the midst of an American success his ideal, which the community calls failure. . . .

The realism of "Arrowsmith" is a return to the realism of "Main Street." In the character of Babbitt, Sinclair Lewis, as it is now clear in perspective, transcended his own limitations and created one of the great type figures of modern literature, a man as human as any fellow mortal and yet significant for American social history. There is no such figure in "Arrowsmith" but instead a gallery of studies of the period, touched with caricature, almost brutal in their naturalism. . . . It is a remarkable selection from the American scene, and need not be sniffed at by the aesthetic because of its Hogarthian exaggeration, and literal reality of detail. This may not be great art, but it is an

*"Fighting Success" by Henry Seidel Canby. From* The Saturday Review of Literature, *I (March 7, 1925), 575. Copyright 1925 by* The Saturday Review of Literature. *Reprinted by permission of the publisher and Mrs. Henry Seidel Canby. Ellipses indicate the omission of portions of the original text.*

invaluable contribution to our knowledge of ourselves and our times; and whatever may be the future of "Arrowsmith" in *belles lettres,* its place in quotation and reference in all histories of our epoch is clearly secure. Furthermore, among these etched caricatures done with such clear and final lines, is one portrait that is much more than satiric caricature. Leora, the first wife of Martin Arrowsmith, who trots along with him like a wise little dog, tactful and plucky and adaptable and humorous even over her own failure ever to be smart or brilliant, Leora is the realist's version of what the American sentimentalist means by "a good pal." Unlike every other person in the crowded story, she lifts above its satire as not being in it for any necessary satiric reason except that she exists so vividly in the imagination of the novelist that he must give her life and place. She is possessive without being predatory, she convinces absolutely like one of Jane Austen's characters without any apparent effort on the part of the novelist to make her convincing. If "Arrowsmith" were not armored and munitioned and speeded for a battleship of satire she would seem more important than all the rest of the crew. Leora, and Babbitt in his later chapters, indicate that when Mr. Lewis grows weary of exposing the world he may, if he will, turn from brilliant social science imaginatively portrayed to pure fiction.

It makes very little difference to me as a reader whether he does or not, and most of the criticisms of Lewis's untempered realism seem to me irrelevant. . . . He is doing a good job where he is. Browning was perhaps rash in asserting that all service ranks the same with God, but it is certainly true that Lewis as a social satirist is eminently serviceable, and that we can well afford to let the future take care of his permanent literary values.

His defects are not literary defects so much as qualities of his particular service. It is true that "nice" people (and there are "nice" people who are neither smug nor stupid nor obscurantist) do not get into his stories. He does not register "nice" people; they do not interest him; and if he were mirroring society instead of satirizing it this would be a prime error. It prevents him obviously from being a Shakespeare, or even a Thackeray, but why should he be either? Stendhal, also, was insensitive to "nice" people. Swift was not, which made him a *rara avis* among satirists. It is time to stop prating of the limitations of Lewis, and on the basis of three of the most remarkable books of our generation give him credit for what with all his faults of narrow vision, insensitiveness to much but not all beauty, obsession with detail, lack of spirituality, and negative philosophy, he undoubtedly is, one of the most brilliant and most serviceable students of society in our times. . . .

"Arrowsmith" is an intensely American novel. The hero is scarcely conscious of another continent except as he touches its spirit in pure science. In spite of his lifelong fight against success, he remains as objective as a guinea pig and as strenuous as a subway. From the first page to the very last, when Martin has tasted of complete worldly success and thrown it all over for happiness in work, there is never any question except as to what he shall *do*. Action is the key to every chapter, every incident. "What shall I *do?*" is written in letters of fire on his brain. What he is, what life is, what he should think, what feel —these are all irrelevant to the story because in his hustling existence there is never any time for them. A Quaker of the seventeenth century or an aristocrat of the eighteenth would marvel at this book, and the society it depicts. Even Gottlieb wonders whether humanity is worth his science. In truth, the philosophy of America as "Arrowsmith" gives it is perhaps more deeply ironical than the author intended. There is essentially no greater clarity of mind in those who like Martin and Gottlieb despise success than in the "Holy Wren" and the cynical Angus who yearn for it. The idealists have no plan except to be always working at their passion. They are just as strenuous, just as irresponsible, just as disregardful of any end except their own pleasure. The difference is solely that Lewis's heroes work at something greater than themselves, while his villains serve their baser instincts. To a saint, or an ascetic, or even to a civilized European all might seem to be mad though with a difference in the morale of their madness.

I suppose that Lewis has been unfair to the medical profession although he has certainly made its heroes stand out with a dignity which no one in "Babbitt" or "Main Street" achieved. I fancy that we who read the book will be for a while unduly suspicious of our physicians. All satires exaggerate—they have to in order to accomplish a satiric effect. Mr. Lewis has called in a scientific man as collaborator so as to direct his pen in unfamiliar ways and insure against too much injustice. But the injustice, if it exists, is not important. . . .

A harsh book, a hard book, in spite of Leora, an illuminating book in a good sense, since it touches upon a universal theme while airing a particular malady, a well written and intensely interesting book in spite of its medical jargon; not a great novel, I suppose, because Lewis knows little of the subtler springs of human nature, and cares less, preferring to grasp the type and let the individual go; and yet a shrewder and more comprehensive satire of American society in the prosperous phase of its materialistic era than anyone else now practising in English is capable of—this much can be said without exaggeration of "Arrowsmith."

## Lucy L. Hazard: The Frontier in Arrowsmith

In *Arrowsmith* we find a progression through the three phases of American pioneering.* The book opens with an apparently irrelevant account—after the much ridiculed manner of old-fashioned novelists— of Arrowsmith's forebears:

> The driver of the wagon swaying through forest and swamp of the Ohio wilderness was a ragged girl of fourteen. Her mother they had buried near the Monongahela—the girl herself had heaped with torn sods the grave beside the river of the beautiful name. Her father lay shrinking with fever on the floor of the wagon box, and about him played her brothers and sisters, dirty brats, tattered brats, hilarious brats. —She halted at the fork in the grassy road, and the sick man quavered, "Emmy, ye better turn down towards Cincinnati. If we could find your Uncle Ed, I guess he'd take us in."
>
> "Nobody ain't going to take us in," she said. "We're going on jus' long as we can. Going West! They's a whole lot of new things I aim to be seeing!"
>
> She cooked the supper, she put the children to bed, and sat by the fire alone.
>
> That was the great-grandmother of Martin Arrowsmith.

That impelling curiosity to see new things persisted in Martin Arrowsmith, brought him back to scientific research after each unsuccessful attempt to stultify his energies and prostitute his purposes, kept him from ever paying wholehearted allegiance to the demand of his superiors for immediate and practical results. In the account of his dedication to abstract science we find a curious overtone of the religious fanaticism of the Puritan frontier. Arrowsmith says of his hero Gottlieb, "His just being in the lab is a prayer." Arrowsmith "exalts the search for fundamental laws above temporary healing as the religious exalts the nature and terrible glory of God above pleasant daily virtues." The fervor of his solitary experimentation finds a natural outpouring in an agnostic prayer:

"*The Frontier in* Arrowsmith" *by Lucy L. Hazard. From* The Frontier in American Literature *(New York: Thomas Y. Crowell Company, 1927), pp. 283-85. Copyright 1927 by Thomas Y. Crowell. Reprinted by permission of the publisher and Brandt & Brandt.*

* That is, the stages of regional pioneering, "primarily concerned with man's attempt to control nature"; then of industrial pioneering, with "man's attempt to control the labor of his fellowmen"; and finally the frontier of spiritual pioneering, "man's attempt to control himself." [R.J.G.]

God give me unclouded eyes and freedom from haste. God give me a quiet and relentless anger against all pretense and all pretentious work and all work left slack and unfinished. God give me a restlessness whereby I may neither sleep nor accept praise till my observed results equal my calculated results or in pious glee I discover and assault my error.

Arrowsmith is like the Puritan pioneers in his contempt for the immediate and practical as compared with the abstract and eternal; in his suspicion that any form is tainted with insincerity; in his ruthlessness toward anything or anybody that gets in the way of his dedication. But while his resemblance to the Puritan is probably one of which he himself was unconscious, he is proudly conscious of his resemblance to the pioneer, so much so that he recurs to that figure to explain his purposes. When his wife seeks to hold him by the old plea of duty to herself and to their child, Martin replies impatiently: "I imagine it's just that argument that's kept almost everybody all these centuries from being anything but a machine for digestion and propagation. The answer is that very few ever do under any conditions willingly leave a soft bed for a shanty bunk in order to remain pure, and those of us that are pioneers . . ." And Arrowsmith whose ancestors were regional pioneers, whose contemporaries commercialize their science in deference to the competitive standards of industrial pioneering, joins his friend on one of "the new frontiers of unwon fields of science" which Professor Turner suggests may take the place of the old frontiers of wilderness.** Like the transcendentalists, Arrowsmith must revert approximately to the conditions of regional pioneering in order to find opportunity for his adventure in spiritual pioneering. Martin Arrowsmith is the most recent incarnation [i.e., in 1927] of that familiar frontier character, the Refugee from Civilization. He and his partner Terry in their cabin laboratory in the woods joyously plan their work—not work for immediate results, for assured profits, for sensational publicity, but long, unrecognized, unremunerative work which may very probably in the end get them nowhere. A new note in American pioneering is struck in this exultant acceptance of failure:

> I feel as if I were really beginning to work now. This new quinine stuff may prove pretty good. We'll plug along on it for two or three years, and maybe we'll get something permanent—and probably we'll fail.

** A reference to the famous "Turner Thesis" about the influence of the physical frontier on the development of American culture and politics. [R.J.G.]

# Chronology of Important Dates

| Sinclair Lewis | Historical Events |
|---|---|
| 1885 Born in Sauk Centre, Minnesota, February 7. | |
| 1898 | Spanish-American War. |
| 1903 Yale College (1903-1908: at Yale; cattleboat trips to England; at Helicon Hall; travels; graduated from Yale, 1908). | Wright Brothers' first airplane flight, Kittyhawk, N. C. |
| 1905 | Rotary Club founded. |
| 1906 | Upton Sinclair, *The Jungle*. |
| 1914 Published first novel, *Our Mr. Wrenn*. Married to Grace Livingstone Hegger. | Outbreak of World War I. |
| 1915 *The Trail of the Hawk* published. | Edgar Lee Masters, *Spoon River Anthology*; Van Wyck Brooks, *America's Coming-of-Age*. |
| 1917 *The Job* and *The Innocents* published. | |
| 1919 *Free Air* published. | 18th Amendment and the Volstead Act (Prohibition). H. L. Mencken, *The American Language* and *Prejudices* (1919-1927); Sherwood Anderson, *Winesburg Ohio*. |
| 1920 *Main Street* published. | 19th Amendment (Woman Suffrage). Eugene O'Neill, *The Emperor Jones* and *Beyond the Horizon*. |
| 1921 | Warren G. Harding, President (1921-1923, "Return to Normalcy"). |

| *Sinclair Lewis* | *Historical Events* |
|---|---|
| 1922  *Babbitt* published. | T. S. Eliot, *The Waste Land*; James Joyce, *Ulysses*. |
| 1923  Caribbean cruise with Paul de Kruif; then at work on *Arrowsmith* in Europe (1923-1925). | Calvin Coolidge, President (1923-1929); Teapot Dome Scandal (1923-1924). D. H. Lawrence, *Studies in Classic American Literature*. |
| 1925  *Arrowsmith* and *Mantrap* published. | Scopes Trial (the "Monkey Trial"). F. Scott Fitzgerald, *The Great Gatsby*; Theodore Dreiser, *An American Tragedy*; John Dos Passos, *Manhattan Transfer*. |
| 1926  First American to decline the Pulitzer Prize. | Ernest Hemingway, *The Sun Also Rises*; Paul de Kruif, *Microbe Hunters*. |
| 1927  *Elmer Gantry* published. | |
| 1928  Divorce; marriage to Dorothy Thompson. *The Man Who Knew Coolidge*. | |
| 1929  *Dodsworth* published. | Herbert Hoover, President (1929-1933); Stock Market Crash (followed by the Depression of the thirties and Roosevelt's New Deal). William Faulkner, *The Sound and the Fury*. |
| 1930  First American to win the Nobel Prize in Literature. In the remaining years Lewis published *Ann Vickers* (1933); *Work of Art* (1934); *It Can't Happen Here* (1935); *The Prodigal Parents* (1938); *Bethel Merriday* (1940); *Gideon Planish* (1943); *Cass Timberlane* (1945); *Kingsblood Royal* (1947); *The God-Seeker* (1949); *World So Wide* (posthumous, 1951). | |
| 1939 | World War II (1939-1945; America entered in 1941). |
| 1942  Second divorce; no remarriage. | |
| 1951  Died in Rome, Italy, January 10. | |

# Notes on the Editor and Contributors

ROBERT J. GRIFFIN, the editor, is a member of the English Department at Yale University and the author of numerous articles, including the essay on Sinclair Lewis in *American Winners of the Nobel Literary Prize* (University of Oklahoma Press).

HENRY SEIDEL CANBY, for many years the editor of *The Saturday Review of Literature,* was one of the authors of *A Literary History of the United States.*

D. J. DOOLEY is a professor of English at St. Michaels College, University of Toronto, and has published a number of articles as well as the book, *The Art of Sinclair Lewis.*

HAVEN EMERSON was a doctor, professor of public health, and author of several works on medicine.

T. R. FYVEL (Raphael Joseph Feiwel) is a British author who has published books on sociology, adolescent delinquency, politics, and Israel.

SHELDON N. GREBSTEIN, who teaches English at Harpur College, State University of New York, has published books on John O'Hara and the Scopes "monkey trial" as well as on Sinclair Lewis.

LUCY L. HAZARD, the author of *The Frontier in American Literature* and *In Search of America,* taught in the English Department at Mills College.

ERIK AXEL KARLFELDT, the Swedish poet and critic, was the Permanent Secretary of the Swedish Academy that chose Lewis for the Nobel Prize.

JOSEPH WOOD KRUTCH has written on subjects as various as Samuel Johnson, Edgar Allen Poe, modern drama, and the Grand Canyon; he was Brander Mathews Professor of dramatic literature at Columbia University.

ROBERT MORSS LOVETT, long a professor of English at the University of Chicago, wrote not only criticism and literary history, but also novels and plays.

H. L. MENCKEN was the famous editor of *Smart Set* and *American Mercury;* a prolific author, his most monumental work was *The American Language.*

EDWIN MUIR was an English novelist, poet, and critic, perhaps best known for his *Structure of the Novel.*

WILLIAM B. OBER is Director of Laboratories at Knickerbocker Hospital and Professor of Pathology at New York Medical College; he has written many articles on the relationships of medicine and physicians with literature and other arts.

LYON N. RICHARDSON, professor of English and director of University Libraries at Western Reserve University, is an editor of *The Heritage of American Literature* and author of *History of Early American Magazines.*

CHARLES E. ROSENBERG has written two books and a number of articles on the social history of medicine and biology; he is a professor of history at the University of Pennsylvania.

MARK SCHORER, who wrote the definitive biography of Lewis, is professor of English at the University of California, Berkeley, and the author of many short stories and critical essays, four novels, and a book on William Blake.

STUART PRATT SHERMAN, author and editor, was professor of English at the University of Illinois and a prolific contributor to periodicals.

CARL VAN DOREN was a well-known editor and the author of numerous books and articles on modern and American literature.

T. K. WHIPPLE wrote *Study Out the Land* and *Spokesmen: Modern Writers and American Life*; he was a professor of English at the University of California, Berkeley.

# Selected Bibliography

Those interested in reading about the whole of Lewis's life and works may want to begin with the four most recent books: Mark Schorer's definitive biography, *Sinclair Lewis: An American Life* (McGraw-Hill Book Company, 1961), which includes a checklist of Lewis's publications; Schorer's collection of critical essays in the Twentieth Century Views series, *Sinclair Lewis* (Prentice-Hall, Inc., 1962); Sheldon Grebstein's estimable critical study in the United States Authors Series, *Sinclair Lewis* (Twayne Publishers, Inc., 1962); and D. J. Dooley, *The Art of Sinclair Lewis* (University of Nebraska Press, 1967). An earlier book by Carl Van Doren, *Sinclair Lewis: A Biographical Sketch* (Doubleday & Company, Inc., 1933), is extremely sympathetic; the appended bibliography by Harvey Taylor is not to be trusted.

The writing of *Arrowsmith* is discussed by both Lewis and his assistant, Paul de Kruif, in *The Designer and the Woman's Magazine* of June, 1924, the issue in which the serialized version of the novel began. Lewis's relevant letters to his publisher are in *From Main Street to Stockholm*, edited by Harrison Smith (Harcourt, Brace & World, Inc., 1952), and De Kruif's rather soured recollections, in *The Sweeping Wind* (Harcourt, Brace & World, Inc., 1962).

The best criticism of *Arrowsmith* is reprinted in this volume. Among the better reviews not included are those by Heywood Broun in the New York *World* (April 10, 1925); Joseph Collins, *The Literary Digest International Book Review* (April); Sherwin Lawrence Cook, *Boston Evening Transcript* (March 7); "R.D.," *The Independent* (March 14); Bernard De Voto, *Evanston New Index* (March 10); and the anonymous English review in *The Spectator* (March 7). Three later, specialized views are Yasuo Hashiguchi, "Arrowsmith and Escapism," *Kyushu American Literature*, No. 8 (1965); Henry Neumann, "Arrowsmith: A Study in Vocational Ethics," *The American Review*, IV (March-April, 1926); and Leon Spitz, "Sinclair Lewis' Prof. Gottlieb," *American Hebrew*, CLVIII (December 3, 1948).